Vasco da Gama

Portrait of D. Vasco da Gama, (1597?) formerly in the Palace of the Viceroys and presently in the Museum of Old Goa. (Glenn J. Ames)

Glenn J. Ames

University of Toledo

Vasco da Gama

Renaissance Crusader

The Library of World Biography

Series Editor: Peter N. Stearns

New York   Boston   San Francisco
London   Toronto   Sydney   Tokyo   Singapore   Madrid
Mexico City   Munich   Paris   Cape Town   Hong Kong   Montreal

Vice President and Publisher: Priscilla McGeehon
Acquisitions Editor: Erika Gutierrez
Executive Marketing Manager: Sue Westmoreland
Production Coordinator: Shafiena Ghani
Senior Cover Design Manager/Designer: Nancy Danahy
Cover Photo: Portrait presumed to be of Vasco da Gama (1469–1524)
    c. 1524, Portuguese School, (16th century) / National Museum of
    Ancient Art, Lisbon, Portugal, / www.bridgeman.co.uk
Senior Manufacturing Buyer: Dennis J. Para
Electronic Page Makeup: Heather A. Peres
Printer and Binder: RR Donnelley and Sons Company/Harrisonburg
Cover Printer: Coral Graphics Services, Inc.

Library of Congress Cataloging-in-Publication Data

Ames, Glenn Joseph
    Vasco da Gama : Renaissance crusader / Glenn J. Ames,
        p. cm. -- (Library of world biography)
    Includes bibliographical references and index.
    ISBN 0-321-09282-1
    1. Gama, Vasco da, 1469-1524--Travel. 2. Explorers--Portugal--
Biography. I. Title. II. Series.

G286.G2A44 2005
910'.92--dc22
[B]   2004048712

Please visit our website at http://www.ablongman.com

ISBN 0-321-09282-1

1 2 3 4 5 6 7 8 9 10—DOH—07 06 05 04

For Miranda and Ethan

Contents

Editor's Preface

"Biography is history seen through the prism of a person."

—Louis Fischer

It is often challenging to identify the roles and experiences of individuals in world history. Larger forces predominate. Yet biography provides important access to world history. It shows how individuals helped shape the society around them. Biography also offers concrete illustrations of larger patterns in political and intellectual life, in family life, and in the economy.

The Longman Library of World Biography series seeks to capture the individuality and drama that mark human character. It deals with individuals operating in one of the main periods of world history, while also reflecting issues in the particular society around them. Here, the individual illustrates larger themes of time and place. The interplay between the personal and the general is always the key to using biography in history, and world history is no exception. Always, too, there is the question of personal agency: how much do individuals, even great ones, shape their own lives and environment, and how much are they shaped by the world around them?

Peter N. Stearns

Author's Preface

Vasco da Gama's life and career have meaning for our own generation for several reasons, not the least of which is the fact that his epic first voyage to India from 1497 to 1499 was a seminal event in creating the global economy and society in which we live today. Many of the economic, political, and religious issues and questions that da Gama confronted in his three voyages to India have great contemporary relevance as well. Da Gama's life (1469?–1524) constitutes above all else the story of the symbiotic rise of a man and his kingdom. In the mid-fifteenth century, the status of both the da Gama family and Portugal were relatively humble. As we shall see, the da Gama family was firmly entrenched in the minor nobility of the province of the Alentejo, while Portugal was seeking to overcome the problems of a small population, poor soil, and frequent Iberian dynastic struggles, in particular with Castile. During the decades of da Gama's life, he, his family, and his kingdom would rise to a position of great wealth, prestige, and power. The architectural treasures of the Monastery of Jéronimos and the Tower of Belém along the banks of the Tagus river in Lisbon today are fitting reminders and legacies of that golden period in Portuguese history.

This incredible shift in fortune was intimately tied to the expansion of the Portuguese Crown and her subjects along the west coast of Africa, India, and eventually the entire Indian Ocean basin during da Gama's lifetime. These conquests created an impressive Asian spice empire called the *Estado da India*, or State of India, which provided social and geopolitical mobility to both da Gama and Portugal. This huge empire, stretching from east Africa to China, and da Gama's career were both grounded on the same solid foundations. These included an impressive nautical knowledge based on a love of the sea and adventure, a toughness and burning desire to overcome adversity engrained in all underdogs, and a ruthlessness and crusading spirit created and nurtured by a supreme faith in the Christian God. The rise of Portugal and da Gama were thus inextricably linked from the imprecise year of his birth to the certain year of his death. From his obscure provincial birth to his well-documented death as first count of Vidigueira and Viceroy of India, his life reflected the rapid and significant changes that Portugal, Europe, and the world underwent during that period.

This volume is subtitled "Renaissance Crusader" because Vasco da Gama's life and career embodied a religious and mercantile crusade that was unique to his country and his time. The fall of Constantinople to the Ottoman Turks in May 1453 symbolically ended the Middle Ages, and the exodus of Byzantine and Greek scholars from that great city to Italy contributed much to the intellectual rebirth, or Renaissance, of Western Europe. At the same time, rising Ottoman power significantly complicated the traditional trade from the Indian Ocean to Europe via the caravan routes and ports of the eastern Mediterranean, a trade the Italian city-states, like Venice, had long dominated. This geopolitical shift furnished additional incentive for the Portuguese Crown to continue the work of **Prince Henry the Navigator.** This most talented son of the first king of the Aviz dynasty, **D. João I,** had overseen voyages exploring the west coast of Africa beginning soon after his able father had conquered the Moroccan coastal town of Ceuta in 1415. This difficult process of exploration ultimately paved the way for the discovery of the sea route to India and its coveted spices.

Da Gama's motivation and methods had evolved from the earlier Western Crusaders of the Middle Ages, who had fought mainly for religious objectives in the Holy Land. By the time of da Gama's birth, both Jerusalem and Constantinople had been lost to Islam, but a new "Holy Land" of sorts beckoned Christian Europe: the riches of India and beyond, combined with the possibility of outflanking Islam and either finding fellow Christians already in those lands or converting the people the Europeans encountered to the "true faith." Da Gama was the product of an emerging Renaissance state, and his "crusade" combined religious and sophisticated economic elements. In the most quoted words of the **Roteiro**, or journal, of his first voyage, he went to India "in search of Christians *and* Spices." The Portuguese Crown desired both, and da Gama, as a loyal servant of the king, demonstrated the true zeal of a crusading warrior in seeking to obtain these objectives throughout his life and career. He was perfectly willing to embrace the ruthless military methods of the Crusades to serve the interests of his king and his faith. In this struggle, the superiority of Portuguese maritime technology and especially ship-borne artillery would greatly assist da Gama's Asian and African successes.

On a more personal level, da Gama would demonstrate a similar single-mindedness and zeal in navigating the complex court politics of a Renaissance court in seeking to advance the interests of his family. As all of the early European explorers and empire builders discovered, including Christopher Columbus and Hernán Cortés, these political waters at home could be extremely difficult to navigate. But da Gama would arguably achieve more lasting rewards for himself and his descendants than any of these contemporaries. In the end, his life and career were notable successes, and his kingdom and his family prospered tremendously.

There are several challenges in writing a biography of Vasco da Gama. The sources available are relatively few and scattered. Most of the manuscript sources are terse, official documents, grants from the Portuguese Crown or mundane business transactions. Few personal writings either were created by da Gama or have survived the ravages of time. Yet, in seeking to overcome the lack of original personal documents written by da Gama, we may find comfort in the cliché that a man's actions speak louder than his words. I believe we can combine the sources that do exist with a careful analysis of his deeds to provide a historically plausible explanation of the forces, both personal and societal, that motivated the man. Since his death, da Gama's life and career have been evaluated by each generation. He has been deified by some and vilified by others. As with any great historical figure, biographies of him frequently say more about the contemporary issues and the historian than the actual events in da Gama's life.

I would like to thank Peter N. Stearns for asking me to contribute this volume for the Library of World Biography series. At Longman, Erika Gutierrez and Doug Tebay have helped tremendously with fine-tuning the project. In Lisbon, I would like to thank Teotonio R. de Souza, my old friend from Goa, for his insights on the project and the Marques Vidal and Sá Fernandes families for making my research trips there productive and enjoyable. The Fundação Calouste Gulbenkian also provided generous financial support that facilitated the completion of this project. I would particularly like to thank Sr. João Pedro Garcia of the Serviço Internacional for his kind assistance. In the United States, I would like to thank Professor Francis A. Dutra of the University of California, Santa Barbara for his sage advice on many issues relating to the military orders in Portugal during this period. My colleague at the University of Toledo, Ted Natsoulas, offered valuable assistance on Africa. Much appreciation goes out to the many reviewers and readers of the book: Charlotte M. Gradie, Ronald Schultz, Morgan R. Broadhead, Chet R. DeFonso, Billy D. Higgins, Robert B. Bruce, Eric Dursteler, Alice-Catherine Carls, David J. Ulbrich, Christopher K. Gardner, James W. Brodman, Rebecca Woodham, Anna Dronzek, Gregory S. Crider, Kerri A. Inglis, Ronald S. Love, and P. A. Mulvey. I also owe thanks to my mother, Janet E. Ames, who read and commented on an earlier draft of the manuscript.

The Life of Vasco da Gama: A Chronology

1469		Da Gama born in the town of Sines
1481		Member of the Military Order of Santiago
1492		Confiscates French shipping on orders of D. João II
1495	December 17–18	Granted Commanderies of Mouguelas and Chouparria
1497	January	Selected to Command First Fleet to India
1497	July 8	**First Voyage to India,** fleet departs from Lisbon
	November 22	Da Gama's fleet rounds the Cape of Good Hope
1498	March 2–29	At Mozambique Island
	April 7–13	Hostile stay at Mombasa
	April 14–24	Stay at Malindi, arranges a "Christian" pilot
	May 20	Reaches Calicut on the Malabar coast of India
	May 28–30	Audiences with the Zamorin of Calicut
	August 29	Departure from Calicut
1499	July–August	Return of *Berrio* and *São Gabriel* to Lisbon
	September	Da Gama **returns to Lisbon** from Azores
	December 24	Provisional grant of lordship of Sines to da Gama
1500	January 10	Da Gama receives right to use title Dom
1500–1501		Marries Dona Catarina de Átaide
1501	March	Created *Capitão-mor* of the Armadas sent to India
1502	January 30	Formally invested as Admiral of the Seas of India
	February 10	**Second Voyage to India,** main fleet departs from Lisbon
	July	Obtains vassalage and tribute from sultan of Kilwa
	September	Captures shipping off Malabar coast, including the *Mîrî*
	November 1–3	Bombards Calicut
	November	Negotiations and trade at Cochin

1503	February 12	Defeats fleet of Zamorin off Calicut
	February 20	Begins return voyage from Cannanur
	October 10	Da Gama **returns to Lisbon** with rich cargo of spices
1504	February 20	Receives royal grants for 400,000 *reais* and 1000 *cruzados*
1507	March 21	Royal decree orders da Gama to vacate town of Sines
1511	November 19	Revenues from Sines and other towns reconfirmed
1513	June 1	Granted right to import goods duty-free from India
1515	August 1	Da Gama given right to hunt in royal preserves in Niza
1515	August 22	Royal permission to send an agent on all India fleets
1518	Early?	Da Gama petitions for title of count
	August 27	D. Manuel responds to da Gama's petition
1519	December 29	D. Manuel grants da Gama the title of count of Vidigueira
1520	January 20	Granted 102,864 *reais* annually as count
1524	January 26	D. João III names da Gama Viceroy of India
	April 9	**Third Voyage to India,** fleet departs from Lisbon
	September 15	Fleet reaches India, anchors at Chaul
	September 23	Da Gama reaches Goa, begins to reform *Estado da India*
	October 21	Sails to Cochin, continues his reforms
	December 24	Da Gama dies on Christmas Eve in Cochin

Finally, a very special thanks as always to Beth, Miranda, and Ethan both for their inspiration and for always providing an interesting and exciting life at home and abroad.

GLENN J. AMES

Vasco da Gama

The Allure of the Sea: Africa and Beyond, 1415–1497

"And this Vasco da Gama was a prudent man, one of good counsel, and of great spirit for all high adventure."
Gaspar de Correia, Lendas da India

Summary

The chapter details how Portugal, a small kingdom with few natural resources, became the leading maritime power in Europe during the fifteenth century. Led by king D. João I, and motivated by religious, economic, and social factors, the Portuguese began exploring the western coast of Africa under the direction of the king's son, Prince Henry the Navigator. Members of the minor nobility in Portugal, like the family of Estêvão da Gama, shared in the spoils of this overseas expansion. Estevão's son, Vasco da Gama, served the Crown well and gained the command of the first voyage charged with discovering the sea route to India in 1497.

Exporting the Reconquista Against Islam to North Africa and Beyond

By the 1460s, the kingdom of Portugal was poised to build on an already impressive record of discovery and conquest it had achieved along the west coast of Africa throughout the earlier decades of that century. In this process, a combination of economic, religious, and social factors had compelled the first king of the Aviz dynasty, D. João I (r. 1385–1433), to extend the *Reconquista* against the Moors. In 1415, D. João, accompanied by his sons, had taken an army from the southernmost province of his kingdom, the Algarve (*al-Gharb*, "the west" of the Muslim world from the eighth century) to North Africa and had conquered the strategic town of Ceuta. This victory began a search for the source of African gold, ivory, and slaves that continued for decades.

The most famous and influential figure in the early years of Portuguese exploration was João's third son, Henry, usually known as Prince Henry the Navigator. Henry organized and funded a series of voyages to explore the African coast beginning around 1418 and continuing until his death in 1460. The obstacles were considerable: centuries of daunting myths and superstitions, nautical difficulties with unknown coastlines and currents, a harsh climate, and jealous European rivals. Portugal herself possessed a relatively small population of about 1.5 million at that point, compared with 18 million for France and 10 million for Spain. It was also a relatively mountainous and arid country with poor soil ill-suited to an age in which agriculture was largely the basis of wealth.

Nevertheless, Henry exploited the advantages the kingdom possessed—a long Atlantic seaboard, fine ports and anchorages, excellent seaman, and a rich seafaring tradition—to overcome these problems. He also provided the logistical, financial, and emotional leadership necessary to coordinate this great enterprise. According to his chronicler, Gomes Eannes de Zurara, Henry wished to learn what lay beyond the Canaries and Cape Bojador; to open profitable new trades and win new converts for Christianity; to investigate the extent of Islamic power; to make alliances with Christian peoples; and to fulfill his horoscope, which compelled him to explore and conquer new lands.

Named Governor of the Algarve in 1419, Henry established himself at the town of Sagres near Cape St. Vincent, the southwesternmost point of Europe, and attracted sailors, cartographers, astronomers, and talented shipbuilders to both his court and his enterprise. In 1420, he was named Grand *Mestre*, or

Master, of the rich crusading military Order of Christ, the successor in Portugal to the knights Templar. During the struggle against the Moors, the Crown had given these military orders huge land grants in return for their assistance in this extended warfare. The Order of Christ, for example, had been given control of over twenty-one towns and more than 400 other jurisdictions, called *commendas,* or commanderies. These territories yielded substantial revenues both to the Order and to the knights or nobles who were granted control over them and their revenues. These knights were known as *commendadors,* or commanders. Using these revenues to underwrite his expeditions, Prince Henry's caravels bore the red cross of the Order of Christ on their sails and had as an additional objective the conversion of pagans to the Christian faith.

In the decades that followed, Prince Henry sent out scores of vessels from the nearby port of Lagos. Explorers under Henry's direction explored the Atlantic islands of Porto Santo and Madeira (1418–1420) as well as the Azores islands and the Canaries. Next, they sailed down the west coast of Africa seeking gold and slaves, eventually proceeding as far as what is now Sierra Leone (1446). Along the way, these men explored the mainland, acquired gold and slaves, and established a fort on an Arguin island off the coast of Guinea (1448). By the time of Henry's death in 1460, Portugal had become the preeminent power in Europe with respect to maritime technology, skills, and overseas exploration. The African coast was quickly yielding its secrets and its trade. More importantly, the quest for gold, slaves, and ivory had become intertwined with the quest for the spices and riches of India.

The Obscure Youth of Vasco da Gama

The decade that began with Prince Henry's death ended with the birth of the man who would culminate the process of Portuguese expansion to Asia: Vasco da Gama. Unfortunately, there are few documents on da Gama's life. His few surviving personal writings relate to everyday business matters. Moreover, the main chroniclers of this period, Barros, Castanheda, Correia, and Goís, frequently offer conflicting evidence on his

Map of Portugal ca. 1500. (Glenn J. Ames)

life. Nevertheless, based on the existing sources, it is possible to construct an acceptable synthesis on the family background and the first twenty-eight years or so of Vasco's life.

By 1415, the year of the conquest of Ceuta, the da Gama family had firm roots in the province of the Alentejo. While the family was neither particularly rich nor of the high nobility, it had a long and honorable history of service to the Portuguese Crown, fighting wars against the Moors and Castile. The family was part of the minor nobility and traced its descent from one Alvaro Annes da Gama, who had fought with distinction in the Reconquest battles of Afonso III. Vasco da Gama's grandfather and namesake carried the royal standard and served with honor in **D. Afonso V's** (r. 1438–1481) war of succession with Castile in the mid-1470s. Initially, the family had ties to the military Order of Aviz and could be found throughout what was known as the Upper Alentejo, close to the frontier with Castile, in and around the towns of Olivença, Elvas, and the provincial center of Évora. It was also linked to the senhorial house of the Prince **D. Fernando,** younger brother of king D. Afonso V. Although Fernando died in 1470, three of his children would subsequently play a large role in the history of Portugal during the formative years of the young Vasco da Gama's life. His daughter Leonor would marry king **D. João II** (r. 1481–1495); his son D. Diogo, who succeeded him as duke of Viseu, would be killed by his brother-in-law; and another son, Manuel, would succeed D. João as king in 1495.

Vasco's grandfather had four sons, and this generation of the family shifted his allegiance to another of the main military orders in the kingdom, the Order of Santiago. His eldest son, **Estêvão da Gama,** was also a *cavaleiro*, or knight, in the household of the powerful D. Fernando. Through these powerful connections and his services in the 1460s and 1470s, Estêvão accumulated a series of income-generating grants. He also married well. His wife, D. Isabel Sodré, was a descendant of Frederick Sudley of Gloustershire, who came to Portugal with the troops of the earl of Cambridge in 1381–82 to fight for the house of Aviz against Castile. The family was also linked to the duke D. Diogo and the Order of Christ. In early Renaissance Portugal, the da Gama family cultivated ties to as many orbits of power and patronage as possible in a quest to rise from the ranks of the minor provincial nobility. The marriage of Estêvão da Gama and D. Isabel Sodré gave the family ties to the four most important sources of institutional patronage in the kingdom: the Crown, the Order of Aviz, the Order of Santiago, and the Order of Christ.

After their marriage, the couple resided in the beautiful coastal town of Sines. Honors and revenues continued to flow to Estêvão. In 1471, he fought in the battle of Tangiers in North Africa and received an annual pension (*tença*) of 7000 *reais* from the Crown. Further services to Afonso V in Morocco and Castile yielded more tangible results. In 1478, the Order of Santiago made Estêvão *alcaide-mor* of Sines and commander of Cercal, towns it controlled. Soon thereafter, he obtained additional revenues from minor taxes in Sines and other nearby towns. In a document from 1481, Estêvão da Gama was listed as one of the thirteen notable members of the Order of Santiago. In 1484, he was reconfirmed in his grants, thus showing he was still alive in that year. Estêvão da Gama then disappears from the existing documentation until ca. 1497, when two of the chroniclers state that he was offered command of the India fleet of that year. Various explanations have been advanced to explain this long gap. The most convincing argument, however, is that Estêvão simply died sometime soon after 1484.

The strategic marriage of Estêvão da Gama and D. Isabel Sodré produced five sons, **Paulo da Gama**, João Sodré, Vasco da Gama, Pedro da Gama, and Aires da Gama, and a daughter, Teresa. Given the lack of birth or baptism records, the best source on the family is a single document from 1480. In November of that year, the bishop of Safim visited Sines. As part of the rituals of the Order of Santiago, he promoted some young men to first tonsure, the ritual shaving of the crown of the head. On the fifth of that month, Vasco da Gama, an illegitimate son of Estêvão, and Paulo da Gama, João Sodré, Pedro da Gama, and Vasco da Gama, his legitimate sons, underwent this ceremony. Vasco da Gama therefore had a bastard half-brother with exactly the same name and probably living in the same house. Because first tonsure usually took place at ten or eleven years of age, Vasco da Gama was probably born in 1469 as opposed to 1460, the other date generally proposed. The place of his birth was probably in Sines.

The exact location was most likely a house near the Church of Nossa Senhora das Salas.

Not much is known of Vasco da Gama's formative years, except that he took the habit of the Order of Santiago in 1481. Most likely, the young da Gama was exposed in Sines to the rich folklore of the sea and to the voyages of discovery that had been undertaken during the days of his grandfather and father. The lure of gold, slaves, ivory, and crusading against the "Moors" was probably strong to a younger son of a minor, albeit rising, noble family. Da Gama probably picked up an acceptable level of practical navigation, along with knowledge of the instruments that were revolutionizing sea travel for the Portuguese, the compass and astrolabe. These instruments in combination with detailed *roteiros,* or sailing instructions kept on previous voyages, and tables detailing the declination of the sun, would later allow da Gama to fix latitude with reasonable precision.

Da Gama probably traveled to Évora, the provincial capital of the Alentejo, during his youth. There he may have pursued more formal studies and certainly witnessed the high culture of that ancient city. He would have seen the palace that King D. Duarte (r. 1433–38) had built to marry his queen in 1421, the ruins of the Roman temple of Diana, and the Church of São Francisco still under construction. Da Gama may even have witnessed the execution of the powerful duke of Braganza in the main square in 1483, a harsh demonstration of the rising power of the young king D. João II. By all accounts, the young Vasco possessed a solid physique and constitution and a steely resolve; he was exceedingly loyal in friendship, terrible in enmity. Overall, it is likely that he spent most of his first twenty years learning the lessons and trade of his father and of Portugal: honing his martial and maritime skills, learning the delicacies of advancing in royal service and in service to the Order of Santiago. As the better documented events of the 1490s demonstrate, he learned these lessons well.

Early Service to the Crown, 1492–1497

The year 1492, when Columbus sailed west in search of Asian wealth in the service of the Catholic monarchs of Castile and

Aragon, Ferdinand and Isabella, also marks the emergence of da Gama from the mists of sparse historical documentation. In that year ships of the king of France, Charles VIII, captured a Portuguese ship returning from São Jorge da Mina on the Guinea coast loaded with gold, even though the two kingdoms were then at peace. In retaliation, according to the chronicler, Gaspar de Resende, D. João II ordered the confiscation of merchandise on French ships then anchored in the ports of Lisbon, Aveiro, Setúbal and the Algarve. The king wrote to "Vasco da Gama, noble of his house and after the count of Vidigueira and admiral of the Indies, a man in which he had confidence and had served in the armadas and naval matters to accomplish these tasks, which he did with great brevity." Charles VIII quickly restored the caravel and its rich cargo to D. João II. This episode shows that as early as 1492, D. João held the young da Gama in high regard with respect to his maritime skills, his ability to lead men, and his willingness to take decisive action. He may have previously demonstrated these skills to the king in the late 1480s and early 1490s by helping to protect the trade of the valuable coastal towns that the Order of Santiago possessed, such as Setúbal, Seisimbra, and Sines, from Atlantic corsairs. During these years, da Gama may have also undertaken voyages to the Atlantic islands, the Guinea coast, or even Flanders, where the Portuguese carried on an extensive trade. The argument that he may have undertaken "secret" voyages for D. João II to the Cape of Good Hope and beyond during this period is much more problematic.

What is clear is that da Gama, young noble of the royal house, knight of Santiago, and resident of Setúbal, served his king well in the French enterprise. At the very least, he accumulated enough royal favor to overcome a more checkered episode that occurred that same year. One night in Setúbal, Vasco and an acquaintance, Diogo Vaz, a squire in the royal household, were walking the streets. There they encountered the *alcaide* João Carvalho and members of the watch. Da Gama was covered in his cape, perhaps against the cold, and was challenged as an evildoer (*malfeitor*). An altercation ensued in which some blows were stuck. Da Gama refused to reveal himself and, according to some sources, shouted "I am not a criminal" as

Views of Church of Nossa Senhora das Salas, Sines. (Glenn J. Ames)

he strode away. The *alcaide* subsequently lodged a formal complaint against both da Gama and Vaz. In his letter of December 1492, D. João II, "wishing to do him grace and mercy," had pardoned Vaz for his violent resistance, fined him 1000 *reais*, and revoked an order for his arrest. Significantly, da Gama was not even cited.

Advances in Navigation and Along the African Coast

The following years were a period of royal transition in Portugal. D. João II, the "Perfect Prince," wanted to establish a more centralized absolutist regime in Portugal. To that end, he crushed the longstanding threat from the nobility by having the most powerful noble in the kingdom, the duke of Braganza, beheaded in 1483. The next year he personally killed his brother-in-law, D. Diogo. D. João II, unlike his father, Afonso V, had also restored direct royal control over the Guinea trade and actively encouraged the process of discovery down the west African coast. In 1482, he built a fortress, which still stands, at São Jorge da Mina, to defend Portuguese economic and political interests along that coast. D. João also oversaw navigational advances. By the 1490s, the Portuguese had added a single meridian line to the traditional **Portolani** charts of the day, which were marked with degrees of latitude. To compensate for the loss of the Pole Star and a lower sun closer to the equator, D. João's Mathematical Council recommended a calculation of latitude with a sun sighting at midday with either an astrolabe or quadrant in combination with a table of declination.

Using these techniques, **Bartolomeu Dias** completed the journey around the southern cape of Africa in 1487–1488. Dias's initial name of the "Cape of Storms" had been changed by D. João II to "Good Hope" in order attract investment in the trade. Wanting as much knowledge as possible about the trading system that awaited the Portuguese in the Indian Ocean basin, the king had also sent two Arab-speaking agents to explore the region via the eastern Mediterranean route in 1487. Afonso de Paiva and Pedro da Covilhã traversed much of the

Middle East, East Africa, and India. The king received a vital report from them written in Cairo in 1490. D. João began preparations for a voyage to India and its coveted spices by ordering three new ships built from trees from his royal estates. In the midst of these preparations, the king died in October 1495.

The royal succession for the "Perfect Prince" had been complicated by the fact that his only legitimate son, D. Afonso, had tragically died from injuries he sustained in a fall from a horse in July 1491 at the age of seventeen. D. João II had an illegitimate son, **D. Jorge**, whom he had named Master of both the Orders of Santiago and Aviz in 1492. But D. João did not have D. Jorge legitimized. Moreover, the Queen, D. Leonor, actively lobbied for one of her surviving siblings to take the throne. In the end, the Crown did indeed go to her brother D. Manuel, duke of Beja. D. João's will, however, asked that **D. Manuel I** (r. 1495–1521) grant even greater powers to D. Jorge. The king wanted his bastard to receive the Mastership of the Order of Christ as well as the title duke of Coimbra. D. Manuel, himself the Grand Master of the Order of Christ since the mid-1480s, predictably refused to hand over this position and its considerable power to D. Jorge. He also delayed granting the title of duke until 1500.

During the initial months of the new reign, Vasco da Gama received two important grants from D. Jorge as Grand Master of the Order of Santiago. On the 17th and 18th of December 1495, da Gama, as "*fidalgo* of the household of the King my Lord and a knight in the Order of Santiago," was granted the commanderies of Mouguelas and Chouparria with all their benefits, rights, rents, and tributes. These were important commendaries not only because they were close to the headquarters of the Order in Palmela, but also because they yielded an annual income of ca. 80,000 *reais*. Clearly da Gama, building on the accomplishments of his father, was a rising personality both at court and in Palmela and merited such recognition. D. Jorge was no doubt anxious to cultivate da Gama's friendship and support, especially at this delicate moment in the realm. Da Gama accepted such patronage willingly, given his attachment to the Order of Santiago, an attachment he would maintain for his entire life. But he was also a rising courtier by the mid-1490s. As such, he also strove to maintain firm ties to D. Manuel, ties that dated back to his grandfather's support of the senhorial house of Viseu, as well as ties to the Order of Christ, which his father had wisely cultivated by marriage with the Sodré family. This lucrative trinity of patronage, if skillfully manipulated, could result in tangible rewards from all three sources, as da Gama's career during the 1490s admirably demonstrates.

At the "Doors of India": Delays and Command of the 1497 Fleet

The most visible sign that Vasco da Gama was both a skillful courtier and a highly respected *fidalgo* of the king's household by this point was his selection in January 1497 to command the long-awaited expedition to India. Dias had returned from his important voyage around the Cape of Good Hope in December 1488. Moreover, as early as 1485, D. João II had informed Pope Innocent VIII that he was at the "doors of India." There were many reasons for the nearly ten-year gap between Dias's voyage and that of da Gama. First, D. João II had waited for accurate intelligence on the Indian Ocean trading network from Paiva and Covilhã, his two Arabic-speaking agents in the Indian Ocean. Second, the campaign in Morocco was especially fierce between 1487 and 1490. Third, the tragic death of the Infante D. Afonso in 1491 no doubt caused him much anguish. Fourth, D. João devoted much time to dealing with the political, religious, and economic fallout in the wake of the arrival of a large numbers of Jews, who sought shelter in Portugal following their expulsion from Spain in 1492.

Perhaps most significantly, Columbus had sailed into Lisbon harbor in early March 1493, claiming to have reached the Indies by sailing west, just as he had promised D. João he would in 1484 when he had offered his services to the Portuguese king. Although D. João received Columbus politely, this unsettling development required further investigation. The new Pope, Alexander VI, who was from Aragon, quickly issued four favorable bulls granting Spain control over the lands Columbus had discovered or would discover to the west. The most famous, the *Inter Caetera*, had proclaimed that all land and sea a hundred leagues west of the Azores and Cape Verde Islands would be a Spanish sphere of exploration. Another bull seemingly extended this sphere to India. Realizing that his chances for a fair hearing in Rome were slim, D. João spent the next few years negotiating directly with Ferdinand and Isabella. In 1494, in a diplomatic triumph for the Aviz king, the treaty of Tordesillas fixed the line of demarcation at 270 leagues further west than the *Inter Caetera*. In doing so, despite what Columbus was erroneously proclaiming to his patrons, this treaty assured Portuguese control over the true ocean passage to India, as well as most of the South Atlantic and, as would soon become clear, Brazil.

D. João II had died the following year; yet another reason for the gap in voyages between Dias and da Gama relates to the delays inherent in the succession of monarchs. D. Manuel devoted a good deal of time in 1496 and 1497 negotiating a marriage treaty with Ferdinand and Isabella for their eldest daughter, Isabel, the young widow of D. Afonso. Perhaps the most important clause of this treaty called for the expulsion of the Jews from Portugal. D. Manuel nevertheless found time to consider questions relating to overseas exploration and discovery, particularly outfitting an expedition for India. In either December 1495 or January 1496, the king called his Council together to debate these questions. According to the chronicler João de Barros, many votes were taken on the issue of India. A majority of the Council favored maintaining the status quo achieved with Tordesillas without exploring the options for further discoveries the treaty allowed. This group argued that the India enterprise should not be attempted given the great obligations and cost it would entail. Such conquests would also lead to a series of new competitors and enemies, as recent events with Castile and Aragon had proven. The other group appealed to the great legacy of Henry the Navigator and the king's father, D. Fernando, arguing that "God will give us the means to preserve the good of the kingdom." In the end, D. Manuel embraced the minority opinion and send an expedition to India.

The need for a skillful commander was a fundamental precondition for the success of this long-discussed and anticipated voyage. Tragically, the documentation on the precise reasons for Vasco da Gama's selection as captain-major (*Capitão-mor*) of the 1497 fleet is very incomplete. Two chroniclers, Barros and Damião de Goís, maintain that Vasco's father, Estêvão, had originally been offered the command by D. João. Because he had died, D. Manuel had then offered it to his son, who had accepted it almost as a right of inheritance. Fernão Lopes da Castanheda claims that the command was originally offered to Vasco's older brother Paulo, who declined based on ill health. He did, however, agree to accompany the fleet "as a captain of one of the ships to advise and assist" the mission. Gaspar Correia, whose version was written later than the others, provides an interesting, although apocryphal, story. "One day as the king sat in his council chamber examining documents, he by chance raised his eyes as Vasco da Gama happened to pass through the room." At that point: "The king felt his heart go into transports as his eyes rested upon Gama." D. Manuel then called da Gama before him and stated: "It would give me great happiness if you would take upon yourself a commission for which I have need of you, [one] in which you will find much travail." Da Gama had then kissed his hand and declared: "Sire, I am already rewarded for any labor that may be, since you ask that I serve, and I shall perform [that service] as long as my life endures."

Why then was da Gama chosen? In this decision, there were personal, political, and social considerations at work. On the personal side, da Gama possessed the physical and psychological requirements for the job. He had a fine physique and constitution and was well versed in the art of warfare. The young *fidalgo* had demonstrated these martial skills in Castile, Morocco, and the streets of Setubal during the 1480s and 1490s. As de Goís noted, "he was a single man of a perfect age to endure the hardships of such a voyage." Da Gama also possessed the requisite nautical skills gained from a life spent largely on the Atlantic coast of Portugal, as well as any formal education he may have had in Évora. He certainly had the reputation for these skills, as his selection and performance in the 1492 affair of impounding the French ships had demonstrated. Da Gama and the other men in his family also had the reputation as hard and, at times, ruthless men, another prerequisite for the position. Mutinies on long ocean passages during this period were common, as both Dias and Columbus could attest. The need to maintain firm discipline from the outset of the voyage was vital. Such discipline demanded harsh, unmerciful punishment. For a man like da Gama, such actions did not pose a problem.

Socially, da Gama's family had risen sufficiently during the previous two generations to merit such a position of command. At the same time, it had not risen so high as to pose any threat to D. Manuel or the senhorial families in the kingdom in the event of his success. The family, thanks to previous meritorious services in Castile and North Africa, was firmly entrenched in the nobility of the royal household, as well as the hierarchy of the Order of Santiago. It also had secure ties to the Orders of Aviz and Christ. It certainly possessed sufficient social standing and noble pedigree to command the small fleet that was to be sent out. Yet, the mission of 1497 was much more than just another voyage of exploration as, for example, had been the case with Dias's fleet. The 1497 expedition was an armed embassy into the largely uncharted political, economic, and religious landscape of the Indian Ocean basin. As a result, its commander would also have to possess the diplomatic skills and social graces required to deal with indigenous rulers along the east coast of Africa and the west coast of India. By the mid-1490s, da Gama had also developed many of these social and diplomatic skills. As his contemporary, Duarte Pacheco Pereira, noted: D. Manuel "ordered Vasco da Gama, commander of the Order of Santiago and courtier at his court, as captain of his ships and men to discover and reconnoiter the seas and lands about which the ancients had filled us with such great fears and dread."

Finally, there were also political factors in da Gama's selection. While there may have been a spirited discussion on the issue of the India voyage by the Royal Council, this was its intended function. No profound and permanent grudges existed at court. After all, the ruling elite in Portugal was a relatively closed caste at this time and had already gained much by the process of expansion. It would potentially gain much more in continuing the process of discovery to India. This same ruling elite, as the da Gama family demonstrated, had fed and would continue to feed from the trough of patronage from all of the military orders of the kingdom. Membership in one did not preclude ties to the others by marriage and less formal forms of association. Politically, in selecting da Gama to lead the expedition, D. Manuel was merely recognizing this fact. Moreover, it was a wise move since in choosing da Gama, D. Manuel wedded the interests of all three Orders to the India venture and the quest for wealth and power for both the kingdom and the nobles serving it. Now all the king had to do was provide Vasco da Gama with a fleet and resources sufficient to carry out this long-awaited voyage.

The Epic First Voyage: Preparations and the Coasts of Africa, 1497–1498

"We left Restello on Saturday, July 8 1497. May God our Lord permit us to accomplish this voyage in his service. Amen!" Roteiro of da Gama's First Voyage

Summary

The chapter details the formation of Vasco da Gama's first fleet for India. It then traces the expedition's course and progress down the African coast and in the South Atlantic to the Cape of Good Hope region by late 1497. Da Gama's initial relations with the indigenous tribal groups of South Africa are described, as are his difficulties on the Muslim dominated Swahili coast during the spring of 1498, especially at Mombasa, where the local sultan ordered an abortive attack on the Portuguese fleet. At Malindi, da Gama would arrange for the services of a skilled pilot to navigate the fleet across the Arabian Sea to India.

The 1497 Fleet: Ships, Manpower, Rations, and Embarkation

Soon after deciding to support the expedition to India, D. Manuel I gave orders to resume work on preparing the ships

17

and materials necessary for the voyage. The king chose Bartolomeu Dias, the skilled mariner who had first rounded the southern tip of Africa, to oversee these tasks. The preparations took place at the royal dockyards along the Tagus River, which flows through Lisbon on its way to the Atlantic. D. Manuel ordered that Dias do his utmost to ensure the success of this difficult enterprise "following what he knew was required, in order to resist the fury of the seas in the vicinity of the great Cape of Good Hope." Dias had already begun work on the design and construction of two of these ships in the reign of D. João II. In doing so, he had modified the classic, shallow draft caravels that the Portuguese had utilized to explore the coast of west Africa in order to create a ship more suited to the storms and pounding of the South Atlantic. The two ships that Dias built were sturdier, heavier vessels called *naus* (ships). They had three masts: the front (fore) and middle (main), rigged with square sails, and the rear (mizzen), rigged with a triangular or lateen sail to facilitate maneuverability. These ships were perhaps 100–120 tons and seventy-five to eighty-five feet long. They had a flat bottom with a high, square stern and bow, which could be used as a fourth mast. The bowsprits carried a carved wooden figurehead of the ship's patron, and their sails carried the red cross of the Order of Christ. The hold was divided into three compartments: the rear, for powder, shot, firearms, and other weapons; the middle, for water casks, extra cable, and riggings; and the forward, for food and other spare equipment. The ships had two decks, with the lower one, like the hold, divided into three compartments for more provisions, trading goods, and gifts for the peoples they encountered. Boards were also attached near the waterline to reduce rolling and pitching in heavy seas. These *naus* had a larger draft and were slower than the caravels, but da Gama and his crews would gain in available space, comfort, and overall seaworthiness on the voyage that awaited them.

To deal with the other usual maritime difficulties, Dias adopted common techniques of the period. To combat barnacles and marine borers, the hulls of these two ships were sealed with a mixture of tallow and pitch or with *cifa*, a thick mixture of tallow and fish oil. Nevertheless, they still needed periodically to be beached and cleaned, or careened; the inside and outsides were scrubbed out and the hull was scraped off and recaulked with a mixture of quicklime, oakum, and oil. The hulls above the waterline were painted with a tarry mixture to preserve the wood. Strips of wood were generally nailed along the seams on the inside of the hulls, as were lead strips to help with protection from the pounding of the waves. Leaks, however, were inevitable, and wooden pumps were generally employed by the crews in order to keep these under control. Heavy planks "two fingers thick" were attached to the sides for protection in fights with other ships, especially those equipped with seaborne artillery. The ships were ballasted with sand, gravel, and stones, the latter used as ammunition as the need arose. The riggings on these two ships were made of flax rope. Only after reaching India would cordage of coir (coconut) be adopted. Each of these ships also carried a longboat rowed by four to six men for trips to shore or exploring inlets.

Both D. João and D. Manuel spared no expense in the construction of these ships upon which so much rested. As Duarte Pacheco Pereira wrote, these ships "were built by excellent masters and workmen, with strong nails and wood; each ship had three sets of sails and anchors and three or four as much tackle and rigging as was usual." The ships were eventually called the *São Gabriel* and the *São Rafael*. By the late spring of 1497, they had been joined by two others in the Tagus. The *Berrio,* of perhaps fifty tons, was a fast caravel with lateen sails. It had been built in Lagos and may have made several voyages along the African coast. D. Manuel had purchased the ship from her owner, Berrios, hence her name. The fourth ship, of perhaps 200–300 tons, was an unnamed storeship purchased from Ayres Correa, a prominent Lisbon shipowner. The average speed of these ships in a favorable wind was probably between six to eight miles per hour. As for armaments, the fleet probably carried some twenty guns. The heavier ones fired a stone shot of several pounds, while the lighter ones, called bombards, were one-pound matchlocks. In battle, the soldiers and crews would use common weapons of the late medieval period: crossbows, spears, axes, swords, javelins, and pikes.

After the major logistical questions relating to the vessels had been addressed, the king called for Fernão Lourenço. Lourenço was an administrator at the House of Mina, "a person in whom he [Manuel] had confidence, and one of no small account, and ordered him to equip the armada and provide it with everything necessary as speedily as he could." To bake sufficient quantities of the mariner's staple, sea biscuit, or hardtack, great ovens were set up. Each man probably received daily rations of about 1.5 lbs. of hardtack, 1 lb. of salted beef or .5 lb. of pork, 2.5 pints of water, 1/3 gill [gill = .25 pint] of vinegar, and 1/6 gill of olive oil. For the Catholic fast days, .5 lb. of rice, codfish, or cheese was given instead of the meat. Each man was also allowed 1.25 pints of wine each day. For a three-year voyage, these rations would have equaled more than 2 tons per person. Unfortunately, these regular rations did not contain the fresh citrus fruits that would combat the most dreaded of the diseases to afflict seamen during this period: scurvy. Experience had already demonstrated to the Portuguese that these fruits were of great value on long ocean trips, although the precise correlation to scurvy may not have been recognized. Yet, the expense involved and storage issues meant that while the officers may have brought along a private stash for their own health, the common seamen and soldiers were dependent on irregular quantities obtained along the way, sometimes with lethal results. D. Manuel ordered spare sails, tackle, and equipment of all kinds, "and in each vessel all kinds of drugs for the sick, a surgeon, and a priest for confession." The trading goods and gifts, consisting of striped cloth, sugar, honey, glass beads, hand basins, red hats, trousers, bells, and tin jewelry, would be judged lacking in most ports along the way. Da Gama sailed with little gold or silver.

While these preparations were underway, da Gama busied himself with the selection and recruitment of his crews. The principal sources for da Gama's first voyage are the accounts of Barros, Góis, Castanheda, and Correia, compiled decades after the fact, and an incomplete journal–logbook, or *Roteiro*, written by a member of da Gama's crew who sailed aboard the *São Rafael*. Two men are the leading candidates for this honor: Álvaro Velho and João de Sá. Velho was a soldier from the town of Barreiro who had spent a good deal of time on the Guinea coast and sailed aboard the *São Rafael*. Sã was a trained notary who later worked at the India House. Yet, since the names of only thirty-one men out of the entire expedition are known, it is plausible that another anonymous author was actually responsible. In any case, no one has disputed the authenticity of the journal.

For his flagship, Vasco da Gama chose the *São Gabriel* and appointed Gonçalo Álvares as its captain. Álvares was a fine sailor who would later hold the important post of pilot-major of the Portuguese empire in Asia, the State of India (*Estado da India*). As the pilot of the *São Gabriel*, da Gama chose Pêro D'Alenquer. D'Alenquer was another wise choice. He had accompanied Dias on his voyage around the Cape of Good Hope. The scribe or clerk of the *São Gabriel* (*escrivão*) was Diogo Dias, the brother of Bartolomeu. Vasco's older brother, Paulo da Gama, captained the *São Rafael*. The pilot of the *São Rafael* was João de Coimbra. João de Sã served as clerk. **Nicolau Coelho**, another tough and experienced sailor, captained the *Berrio*. Coelho would sail to India again in 1500 and 1503 and receive a fine pension of 70,000 *reais* and a coat of arms from D. Manuel in 1500. His pilot was Pêro Escolar, who would receive a pension of 4000 *reais* from the king in 1500: "for the service . . . [he] has performed for us both in the regions of Guinea and in the discovery of the Indies, where we sent him." The clerk of the *Berrio* was Álvaro de Braga, who would eventually head the Portuguese factory at Calicut and be rewarded a pension by D. Manuel in 1501. As captain of the unnamed storeship, da Gama appointed one of his retainers, Gonçalo Nunes.

Because the voyage would involve interaction with African tribes, Arabs, and Indian states, two interpreters were recruited. Martin Afonso had lived in the Congo for some time and knew the dialects of several Bantu tribes. Fernão Martins had spent several years as a captive of the Moors and spoke fluent Arabic. The Chaplain and Father Confessor was Pedro de Covilhã. Ten convict-exiles, or *degredados,* were also sent out aboard the fleet. According to Góis, these men were "seized for mortal crimes and whose misdeeds the king pardoned so that they

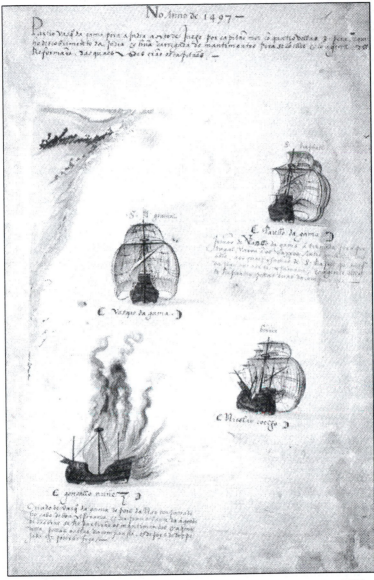

Fleet of Vasco da Gama that Discovered the Sea-Route to India, 1497, from the *Memória das Armadas* (Lisbon, 1567.) (Glenn J. Ames)

might serve on this voyage, and he granted them grace and mercy, giving them a chance as persons who might prolong their lives, no matter in what manner." According to Correia, Vasco da Gama requested these men "to adventure to leave them behind in desolate lands, where, if they survived, they might prove of value to him when he returned and found them again." Perhaps the most interesting convict was João Nunes, a New Christian, or recently converted Jew, who knew some Arabic and Hebrew and remained in India after da Gama's departure. According to Correia, "he was a man of keen intellect, who could understand the language of the Moors [natives of Calicut] but could not speak it."

There are various estimates on the exact number of men who sailed aboard the four ships. Girolamo Serengi, a merchant from Florence living in Lisbon, gave the number of 118 in a much-cited letter of the summer of 1499. The chroniclers Góis, Castanheda, and Osório all gave the number of 148. Gaspar Correia offered the highest estimate of around 260. The generally accepted figure has been the one provided by João de Barros of 170, with seventy on the flagship *São Gabriel*, fifty in the *São Rafael*, thirty in the caravel *Berrio*, and twenty in the storeship. On the *São Gabriel*, the crew probably included a master, pilot and underpilot, mate boatswain, twenty able seamen, ten ordinary seamen, two cabin boys, a master gunner, eight bombardiers, four trumpeters, the clerk, a storekeeper, a master-at-arms, the surgeon, two interpreters, the chaplain, six artificers (carpenter, caulker, cooper, ropemaker, armorer, and cook), and perhaps ten servants. Da Gama strove to find the best men available for his crews, and D. Manuel allowed him to choose from among "the best and most skillful pilots and mariners in Portugal." During the spring of 1497, da Gama spent a good deal of time with his men, encouraging them to improve their nautical skills. For those who did, he increased their pay by two-fifths. According to Duarte Pacheco Pereira, "they received, besides other favors, pay higher than that of any seamen of other countries." D. Manuel and da Gama were both clearly determined to give the expedition every chance of success.

During these months, da Gama also arranged for the maps, charts, and instruments he would need for the voyage. He was greatly assisted by the accumulated knowledge of previous Portuguese voyages dating back to the days of Prince Henry. A vast store of carefully guarded maps, charts, and letters was available in Lisbon. This documentation included reports brought to Lisbon by an Abyssinian priest, Lucas Marcos, in 1490. Marcos's reports probably included the famous letter from Cairo of Pedro de Covilhã. If so, da Gama would have possessed at least a rudimentary knowledge of the trading system of the Indian Ocean basin and the major political powers and ports on the east coast of Africa and the western coast of India upon his departure.

To assist da Gama and his pilots in navigation, a store of compasses, at least two astrolabes, and quadrants were taken. There had been references to the compass as early as the twelfth century in Europe, with most crediting its invention to the Italians. In the *Roteiro*, it was referred to as the Genoese (*genoisca*) needle. The compass cards of da Gama's day were vastly different from those used today. Given the high illiteracy rates, instead of number and letters on these cards, the points were given in different shapes or colors radiating from the pivot point in the center. The Portuguese called the cards the "rose of the wind" (*rosa dos ventos*). Although portable timepieces were being produced in late fifteenth-century Germany, they were not particularly reliable, and da Gama's fleet kept time using large (1 hour) and small (30 minutes) hourglasses. Each time the ship's boy turned the glass, a bell was rung. Eight bells with the small glass, equaled four hours, the standard time for one watch. The astrolabe (in Arabic *asthar-lab* or "to take a star") had also proven of great value to the Portuguese on their voyages of discovery. This instrument was essentially a flat wooden or brass circle etched along the edges in degrees and minutes with two sights for reading celestial bodies. Used in conjunction with tables of declination provided in works like Zacuto's *Almanach Perpetuum Celestium*, the astrolabe could provide fairly accurate readings of latitude. One last bit of cargo was far heavier than these instruments: D. Manuel ordered three stone *padrões*, or columns, with the royal crest of Portugal embarked. These large stone monuments were named the "São Gabriel," the "São Rafael," and the "Santa Maria." Da Gama would erect them to signal further conquests for the Portuguese Crown.

To escape the summer heat of Lisbon, D. Manuel held court in early July 1497 in Montemor-o-Novo, eighteen miles west of the capital. Vasco da Gama and his officers were summoned to this ancient town, dominated by an old Moorish castle, for their formal farewell. It was a solemn occasion with great pomp and lavish display. All of the leading nobles of the realm were present in their finest dress, as was the hierarchy of the Catholic Church in their ceremonial robes and symbols of power. According to João de Barros, D. Manuel declared, "I, pondering much on what might be the most profitable and honorable enterprise, and one worthy of much glory in which I might undertake to carry out . . . I have come to the decision that no other is more proper for this my kingdom . . . than the search for India and the lands of the East." What did the king hope to achieve with this new conquest? "I hope that in the mercy of God that not only may the faith of Our Lord Jesus Christ His son be proclaimed and received through our efforts, and that we may obtain the reward thereof—fame and praise among men—but in addition kingdoms and new states with much riches, wrested by force of arms from the hands of the barbarians." Why had he selected da Gama for this vital mission and crusade? "I have in my mind how Vasco da Gama, who is here present, has given a good account of himself in all matters which were entrusted to him, or with which he was charged. I have chosen him for this journey, as a loyal cavalier, worthy of such an honorable enterprise."

Da Gama kissed the king's hand and D. Manuel then presented him with a silken banner with the cross of the Order of Christ in the center. In response, the Captain-major declared: "I, Vasco da Gama, who now have been commanded by you most high and powerful king, my liege lord, to set out to discover the seas and lands of India and the Orient, do swear on the symbol of this cross, on which I lay my hands, that in the service of God and for you I shall uphold it and not surrender it in the sight of the Moor, pagan, or any race of people that I may encounter, and in the face of every peril of water, fire, or sword, always to defend and protect it, even unto death." The Captain-major also swore to follow "with all fidelity, loyalty, watchfulness, and diligence" the written orders given to him for the mission until the time when he could return "to this place where I now stand, in the presence of your Royal Highness, with the help of the grace of God, in whose service you are sending me." At that point, da Gama received his formal instructions along with letters from D. Manuel to the rulers that might be encountered on the voyage, including the semi-mythical Christian king Prester John and the king of Calicut. The following day, a mass was celebrated. Da Gama and his officers then departed by horse for Lisbon to meet up with their ships and crews.

On July 7, 1497, the four ships of the fleet lay at anchor off the suburb of Restello, four miles west of the arsenal of Lisbon where the Tagus widens on its way to the sea. At this site, Prince Henry had long before ordered built a small chapel dedicated to St. Mary of Bethlehem (Belém). It was common for Portuguese mariners to say their prayers for a safe and successful voyage in this chapel. Vasco da Gama, his brother Paulo, and his other officers spent most of that night in the chapel, confessing their sins and praying for strength to overcome the obstacles they would confront in this great enterprise. The next morning, a final mass was held. At this service, the priest, based on a bull of Pope Martin V, offered general confession and absolution to any member of the fleet who lost his life in this holy venture. All of the officers and crews were in their formal clothing, the armor of the officers and soldiers shone in the hot summer sun, and the ships flew every flag they possessed. In this setting, the final good-byes were said with family members with great emotion. According to Barros, the area in front of the chapel could have been called the "shore of tears." Da Gama and his crews boarded their ships and, when a favorable wind rose late in the afternoon of July 8, the fleet departed. The voyage to culminate the quest of Prince Henry and D. João II was at last underway. Da Gama was probably twenty-eight years old, of a solid constitution and medium stature, intelligent, single-minded, and, when required, vicious. In short, he was the ideal commander for the challenges ahead.

From Lisbon to the Cape of Good Hope, July–November 1497

The first stage of the voyage was uneventful. On July 15, the Canary Islands were sighted. A dense fog off the *Rio do Ouro* (River of Gold) on July 16 separated the ships for a time. Da Gama, however, had given orders for a rendezvous at the Cape Verde Islands, and by July 27 all four ships were at anchor in the bay of Santa Maria, the harbor of Santiago, the largest of these islands. There, the fleet was joined by a ship under the command of Bartolomeu Dias, who had been ordered by the king to accompany da Gama on the initial stage of the voyage. Dias had been appointed to the captaincy of the fort at São Jorge da Mina as a reward for his services, and he was sailing to take up that post. He provided da Gama with some final insights on navigating the South Atlantic and the Cape of Good Hope. At Santiago, the fleet took on meat, water, and wood and did the much-needed repairs. The ships departed on August 3, and, in the words of Barros, "leaving the said island, Bartholomew Dias, who had accompanied them until then set a course for Mina, Vasco da Gama set his own."

On August 18, some 200 leagues from Santiago, the main yard of the *São Gabriel* broke in a storm, and it took two days to repair. Instead of hugging the African coast to cover the 3,300 miles to the Cape of Good Hope, da Gama and his fleet boldly changed course, heading west out from Sierra Leone, and made a wide circular swing toward the as-yet-unknown coast of Brazil. Da Gama made this seemingly radical shift in course because, based on previous Portuguese voyages in the South Atlantic, he knew that such a course would yield the quickest voyage to the Cape. He would also avoid the contrary coastal winds and currents that had frustrated earlier expeditions along the African coast during a good part of the fifteenth century. Da Gama probably sailed southwest from Africa to approximately five degrees north latitude, continued to within a short distance of Brazil, and then swung around to a course of east-southeast at approximately twenty degrees south latitude.

In doing so, he obtained the best winds and currents for the voyage to the Cape of Good Hope and established a route that sailors would follow for the next four centuries. Nevertheless, it was a long and difficult voyage. The fleet sailed out of sight of land for nearly three months, the longest such passage by a European to that time. As the poet **Luis Vaz de Camões** later described this part of the voyage: "we saw no more than sea and sky." It was an epic maritime achievement, one that makes Columbus's five-week jaunt across the Atlantic from the Canaries to the Bahamas pale by comparison. Whales and seals were finally sighted on October 27. According to the *Roteiro*, "On Saturday, the 4th of the same month [November], a couple of hours before break of day we had soundings in 110 fathoms, and at nine o'clock we sighted land." The four ships came together and fired a salute to celebrate their safe arrival on the African coast once again.

Initial Contacts with the Khoikhoi and Nguni in the Cape Region

D'Alenquer, however, could not identify their precise location in relation to the Cape, so the fleet stood out to sea for three more days. Finally, on November 8 they anchored in Saint Helena bay, where the crews spent eight days, "cleaning the ships, mending the sails, and taking in wood." Some fresh water was also found in a nearby river, which da Gama named Santiago. D'Alenquer's problem in fixing their exact location confirmed a shortcoming da Gama had already noted: the imprecise readings of the sun's altitude that had been made shipboard due to the pitching and rolling of the ships and the limitations of his instruments. So, the Captain-major went ashore to take more precise readings.

During the stay at Saint Helena, the Portuguese had contact with the various tribesmen of that region, especially the Khoikhoi. The ancestors of these Khoisan-speaking people had acquired substantial numbers of cattle in northern Botswana, and their culture centered upon livestock breeding. The Khoikhoi had also learned to forge metals, and, beginning about 1300, they had then spread south to the Cape region, usually in individual clan organizations numbering in the hundreds that may have been part of larger, loosely structured political groups. By 1488, they had not only reached southernmost Africa, but in doing so they had affected the culture of the Bantu speakers already entrenched there, including the Nguni.

Da Gama and his men, of course, were not concerned with internal African migrations and cultural interaction at this point. Their description of the Khoikhoi was brief: "[they] are tawny-colored. Their food is confined to the flesh of seals, whales, and gazelles, and the roots of herbs." They dressed in skins "and wear shealths over their virile members." On November 9, one Khoikhoi was captured while gathering honey. He was taken aboard the *São Gabriel* and given food and clothing and then sent back to his village. The following day, fifteen more appeared and bartered some goods with the Portuguese. Da Gama showed them the goods he was seeking on his voyage, including spices and gold "but it was evident that they had no knowledge whatever of such articles." Consequently, they were given "round bells and tin rings." This cultural interaction continued on November 12, when fifty more "natives made their appearance." Once again, relatively friendly bartering took place with the Khoikhoi. The author of the *Roteiro*, for example, traded a copper coin worth less than a penny for shell earrings, a foxtail fan, and a sheath. This transaction demonstrated the value the Khoikhoi placed on copper. ". . . indeed they wore small beads of that metal in their ears."

That same day, one of the crew, Fernão Velloso, asked for permission to accompany the Khoikhoi ashore. At the behest of Paulo da Gama, the Captain-major granted this request, a decision he would soon regret. Not long afterwards, after sharing a roasted seal with them, Velloso somehow offended them and was spied by da Gama and others running for his life toward the surf. Although the crew managed to load Velloso into a longboat and save him, the Khoikhoi threw stones and fired arrows, wounding Vasco da Gama in the leg. Several other Portuguese were also wounded in this skirmish, including Gonçalo Álvares, the master of the *São Gabriel*. Up to that point, da Gama had assumed that the Khoikhoi posed no threat, and the crews had landed without weapons. After this attack, the

Captain-major ordered some of his crossbowmen ashore to "teach them a lesson."

On November 16, the fleet set sail once again. In a fairly accurate estimate, D'Alenquer believed that they were thirty leagues from the Cape of Good Hope. Da Gama ordered a course to the south-southwest and "late on Saturday [November 18] we beheld the Cape." Contrary winds, however, prevented the fleet from actually doubling the Cape until Wednesday, November 22. The goal of the preceding five months had at last been achieved. This stage of the voyage had been a stern test of da Gama's abilities as a commander and mariner. He had overcome the winds, currents, and violent storms of the South Atlantic, and in doing so had won the respect of his crews. He was not only an impressive seaman but a fine leader of men. D. Manuel, it appeared, had chosen wisely. Yet the challenges of the voyage were only beginning.

On November 25, 1497, St. Catherine's Day, da Gama's fleet anchored in the bay of São Bras (Mossel Bay). Dias had called this place "Herdsmen's Bay" and killed one of the "natives" with a crossbow ten years previously. The fleet remained there for thirteen days. During that time, some water and wood were taken on. Da Gama also had the storeship of the fleet broken up and her provisions distributed among the other vessels. Here, da Gama probably had his first contact with the Nguni speaking people of the eastern Cape region. The Nguni were recently established along this coast and the pastureland located slightly inland. They were both herdsmen and cultivators of millet and other crops who lived in small villages obeying chiefs called *nkosi*. On December 1, about ninety Nguni appeared on the shore. Da Gama landed with an armed party and engaged in some bartering with them. "When close to shore the captain-major threw them little round bells, which they picked up."

The next day, about 200 Nguni appeared and brought "a dozen oxen and cows and four or five sheep." These men also brought their pipe instruments and began to play and dance. Vasco da Gama enjoyed this show and ordered his trumpeters to join in from the Portuguese ships. He then returned to the *São Gabriel*, where he told the other musicians to join in. To the astonishment of all, da Gama even danced with the crew. Either this action was a reflection of the joy he felt at doubling the Cape, or perhaps it was a calculated move to cultivate support of the crews for the difficulties ahead. In any case, after the music and dancing ceased, some Portuguese officers landed ashore and bought a black ox for three tin bracelets. "This ox we dined off on Sunday. We found him very fat, and his meat as toothsome as the beef in Portugal."

Yet this apparent cordiality did not last. The following day, December 3, a dispute arose over the Portuguese appropriation of water. In response, da Gama ordered his men to land with weapons at the ready "wearing our breastplates, for he wanted to show that we had the means of doing them an injury, although we had no desire to employ them." To emphasize this point, the Captain-major "ordered two bombards to be fired from the poop of the long boat." This demonstration of artillery, even small-caliber artillery, had a profound effect on the Nguni and they fled. In point of fact, this initial demonstration of the technological advantages in artillery, and especially shipborne artillery, that the Portuguese enjoyed would herald the coming of the empire they would establish in the Indian Ocean basin during da Gama's lifetime.

On December 7, the fleet finally departed from São Braz. Da Gama left behind one of the stone *padrões* embarked by D. Manuel and a large cross made from wood from the old storeship. Fittingly, given events in the bay, "when about to set sail, we saw about ten or twelve blacks, who demolished both the cross and the pillar before we had left." On December 16, the ships passed the last *padrão* erected by Dias on his voyage and entered waters never before navigated by Europeans. Da Gama and his fleet spent the rest of December sailing along the eastern coast of Africa, working against the Agulhas current.

By Christmas Day 1497, some seventy leagues had been explored past Dias's furthest point, and the Captain-major called this land Natal (Christmas). The ships had been at sea continuously for three weeks, and not that much water had been taken on at São Braz. As a result, "drinking water began to fail us, and our food had to be cooked with salt water. Our daily ration of water was reduced to a *quartilho* [three-quarters of a pint]. It thus became necessary to seek a port." On January 11, 1498, the three remaining ships anchored near a small river. The people who came to greet them here were also probably Nguni. Martin Afonso, who had lived in the Congo, was sent ashore, where he discovered that, using his Bantu dialects, he could communicate with them fairly well. "They were tall people, and a chief ('Senhor') was among them." Da Gama sent the *nkosi* "a jacket, a pair of red pantaloons, a Moorish cap, and a bracelet." The chief in turn "said that we were welcome to anything in his country of which we stood in need: at least this is how Martin Afonso understood him." Afonso accompanied the chief to his village and was well received. He reported that the country was "densely peopled"; the people were farmers who lived in straw huts; they used longbows and iron-tipped arrows and spears for weapons and wore copper armlets and anklets. Thanks to the elephants in the region, some of the men even carried daggers in ivory sheaths. The Nguni also evaporated seawater for salt. Due to the friendly reception, da Gama called this region the "Land of Good People" and named the river the Copper River. The ships were able to take on wood and water before departing.

On January 25, 1498, the fleet entered the mouth of the Quelimane River and remained there for over a month. The Nguni also populated this region: "These people are black and well made. They go naked, merely wearing a piece of cotton stuff around their loins. . . . The young women are good looking. Their lips are pierced in three places and they wear in them bits of twisted tin." The Nguni brought water and vegetables to the ships. A few days later two chiefs of the country appeared. "They were very haughty, and valued nothing which we gave them." One of these chiefs wore a cap with a silk embroidered fringe, and the other stated that he came from "a distant country, and had already seen big ships like ours." Although these chiefs were aloof and were not impressed with his gifts, da Gama saw their clothing and familiarity with his ships as a sign he was at last approaching India and that traders from Asia had certainly visited this part of the African coast. Thinking he was nearly at the end of his voyage, da Gama called the river the "River of Good Signs."

During this stop, the Portuguese once again careened their ships, repaired a mast on the *São Rafael*, and took on water. Unfortunately, a lack of citrus fruit and vitamin C finally brought on the first outbreak of scurvy. According to the *Roteiro*: "Many of our men fell ill here, their feet and hands swelling, and their gums growing over their teeth, so that they could not eat." During this crisis, Paulo da Gama acquitted himself well; he visited and tended the sick and shared "generously those things for the relief of the illness which he had brought with him for his own use." Fresh citrus was evidently obtained, because the scurvy soon disappeared. At the River of Good Signs, Vasco da Gama erected a *padrão*, named after the ship that had carried it from Lisbon: the *São Rafael*. On February 24, the fleet departed.

The Reach of Islam: A Mixed Reception on the Swahili Coast

Sailing northeast for approximately 300 miles, da Gama's expedition made its way up the Mozambique Channel between Africa and Madagascar. On Friday morning, March 2, 1498, the island of Mozambique was sighted. Once the ships had anchored in the roadstead, "there approached seven or eight of them [boats], including canoes, the people in them playing upon *anafils* [Arabic, *El-nafir*, a type of trumpet]." Da Gama had finally reached the part of the Swahili-speaking East African coast where Islam had made strong inroads in the preceding centuries. From the outset, the Captain-major recognized his hosts as Muslims. A few may have been transplanted traders from Arabia, but the vast majority of the people were Swahili-speaking Africans. Nevertheless, the political, economic, and religious hierarchy of the Muslim city-states that dominated this coast also had a good knowledge of Arabic as well. Many of the elite had made their pilgrimage or *hajj* to Mecca, and Arabic was the language of the Koran and the call to prayers. According to the *Roteiro*: "The people of this country are of a ruddy complexion and well made. They are Mohammedans, and their language is the same as that of the Moors."

During the fourteenth and fifteenth centuries, the economic, political, and religious power of Islam had expanded throughout the Indian Ocean, creating in the view of some an "Islamic world-economy" in the region. While this view may be exaggerated, there can be little doubt that Muslim traders dominated a sizable portion of the trade and trading networks from East Africa to Indonesia. One vital link in this network was the rich triangular trade that was then flourishing between Gujarat in western India, the Red Sea ports, and East Africa. The African terminus of this trade was dominated by independent Muslim city-states, with the sultanates of Kilwa, Mombasa, and Malindi the most powerful. A common religion may have tenuously linked these states, but economic and political rivalry was endemic.

The richness of this trade was obvious even at Mozambique island. "Their dresses are of fine linen or cotton stuffs, with variously colored stripes, and rich and elaborate workmanship. They all wear *toucas* [scarves] with borders of silk embroidered with gold." Upon their arrival, da Gama discovered that four Muslim ships were in port, "laden with gold, silver, cloves, pepper, ginger, and silver rings, as also with quantities of pearls, jewels, and rubies, all of which articles are used by the people of this country." Clearly, the expedition had at last found the long-sought wealth and riches of the East and the enemy of the Christian Reconquest as well.

Using his Arabic-speaking interpreter, Fernão Martins, da Gama learned that the fleet might be close to finding eastern Christians as well. Even the kingdom of the elusive Christian king Prester John in Africa might soon be found. The Captain-major was told that further along the coast "there were many cities . . . and also an island, one half of the population of which consisted of Moors and the other half of Christians, who were at war with each other. This island was said to be very wealthy." As for Prester John, he "resided not far from this place; that he held many cities along the coast, and that the inhabitants of those cities were great merchants and owned big ships." The residence of Prester John was said to be far in the interior and "could be reached only on the backs on camels." This information made the Portuguese "so happy that [they] cried with joy and prayed God to grant us health, so that we might behold what we so much desired."

Da Gama's reception on Mozambique island suggests that, at least initially, the local sultan, called sheikh Zacoeja (Shah Khwajah?) by Barros, did not recognize the Portuguese as Christians and may have even believed they were Muslims. The Captain-major did not dissuade him. He utilized this grace period to gain as much information as he could about the trading products and networks of the region. Da Gama was also acquainted with the alternating monsoons that dictated all sailing in the Indian Ocean. The northeast monsoon (January–March) permitted Arab traders to sail from India, Persia, and Arabia to East Africa in the "winter," and the southwest monsoon (June–September) facilitated their return home in the "summer." Da Gama also studied the construction of the Muslim ships, or *dhows*. "The vessels of this country are of good size and decked. There are no nails, and the planks are held together by cords, as are also those of their boats. The sails are made of palm-matting. Their mariners have Genovese needles, by which they steer, quadrants, and navigating charts." The Portuguese also saw coconut palms on the island and began to appreciate the importance of this tree.

Initial relations with the sultan were cordial. He visited both the *Berrio* and *São Gabriel*, dined with Vasco da Gama, and even entertained the Portuguese in his residence. The rather paltry quality of the gifts da Gama carried with him began to reveal itself on Mozambique island. Nicolau Coelho had presented the richly dressed sultan with a red hood. Reflecting the sophistication of Muslim culture and cuisine at this time, the sultan in return sent Coelho a jar of dates made into preserves with cloves and cumin seeds. Da Gama could offer little more. "The Captain-major gave him many good things to eat, and made him a present of hats, *marlotas* [short dress made of wool], corals and many other products." Not surprisingly, the sultan "however, was so proud that he treated all we gave him with contempt, and asked for scarlet cloth of which we had none."

During the stay on Mozambique island, two "Christian" captives from India were also brought aboard the *São Gabriel*.

As soon as they saw the figurehead of the angel Gabriel, they fell to their knees and began to worship this image. The Portuguese were overjoyed, thinking they had found Christian brethren. These captives were in fact Hindus whose religion embraced the images of their many Gods. The Portuguese, from this point of the voyage, consistently mistook Hindus for members of a lapsed eastern Christian sect. Beginning with Prince Henry, one of the fundamental objectives of Portuguese overseas expansion had been to find such Christians beyond the land of the Moors. Da Gama, therefore, was intent on finding Christians around the Indian Ocean basin. In doing so, he probably used a simple process of elimination: These captives were not like the pagans, heathens, or barbarians he had already encountered; they were certainly not Muslims; they most certainly had worshipped a Christian image; therefore, they must have been Christian. This is what Vasco da Gama wanted to believe, and this is what he did believe. It was a conviction that he would retain for the remainder of the voyage. One outcome of this scene aboard the *São Gabriel* was that the sultan was definitively disabused of any notions he may have held regarding the religion of the men aboard these ships. As a result, tensions rose daily in early March 1498. As the writer of the *Roteiro* described: "but when they learnt that we were Christians they arranged to seize us and kill us by treachery. The pilot, whom we took with us, subsequently revealed to us all they intended to do, if they were able."

By this point in the voyage, da Gama had already decided to arrange for an Arab or Indian pilot to guide his ships across the last sizable stretch of unknown ocean on the route to India: the Arabian Sea. Even in this climate of growing mistrust, he invited the sultan to dine aboard the *São Gabriel*. At this meeting, da Gama arranged for two pilots. The terms he negotiated with them reflected his justifiable suspicions. He paid them each thirty **misqâls** in gold (1 *misqâl*=ca. 470 *reais*) and two shawls, "on condition that from the day on which they received this payment one of them should always remain on board if the other desired to go on land." Nevertheless, tensions continued to mount, and on March 10 da Gama removed his anchorage

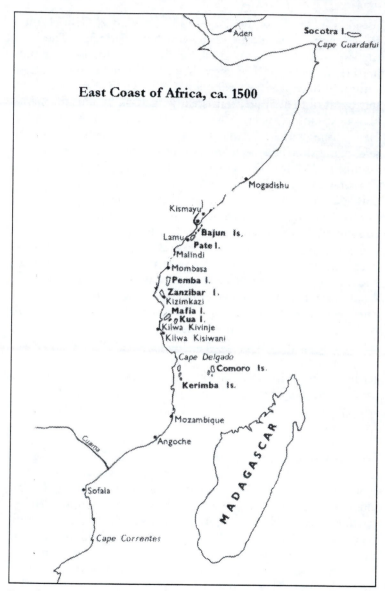

East African Coast, ca. 1500. (Glenn J. Ames)

to the islets of São Jorge, well out in the bay. One of the pilots had already fled, and da Gama and Coelho took two boatloads of armed men to look for him. As they rowed toward the town, Muslim boats carrying archers attacked their longboats. The Portuguese returned fire, and the appearance of Paulo da Gama in the *Berrio* with even more firepower decided the issue.

On March 11, a mass and communion were held, and the fleet departed, "taking with us many fowls, goats and pigeons, which had been given us in exchange for small glass beads." Contrary winds, however, prevented headway, and by the March 15 da Gama's ships were again anchored off the islets of São Jorge. The sultan sent out an envoy: "His ambassador was a white Moor [Arab] and sharif [descendant of the prophet Muhammed] that is a priest, and at the same time a great drunkard." Although this envoy feigned peaceful intentions, the two sides soon came to open hostilities over the issue of resupplying the fleet with water. On March 24, the sultan warned da Gama not to attempt to take on this badly needed commodity. "The Captain-major no sooner heard this [threat] than he resolved to go, in order to show that we were able to do them harm if we desired it." Da Gama loaded all of his boats with armed men and mounted small artillery in their poops. Although the sultan had constructed palisades of planks, they were routed by the Portuguese bombardment. Da Gama fired stone shot at the town for three hours, "when we were weary of this work we retired to our ships to dine."

After dinner, da Gama ordered his longboats back out in order to search for prisoners, whom he wanted to exchange for the two "Christian" captives and a black slave of João de Coimbra, the pilot of the *São Rafael*, who had escaped to town. That night, Paulo da Gama's boat captured one dugout loaded with four African Muslims. Two others dugouts were also captured, including one boat belonging to the sharif. One of the escaped pilots, both of them having fled by that point, was also recaptured. These boats yielded "fine cotton-stuffs, baskets made of palm-fronds, a glazed jar containing butter, glass phials with scented water, books of Law [including the Koran], a box containing skeins of cotton, a cotton net, and many small baskets filled with millet." Vasco da Gama kept the Koran to show to D. Manuel and distributed the rest as spoils of war to his officers and crews. The next day, the Portuguese were able to take on water without opposition, and on March 25 bombarded the town once again.

Finally, on March 29, the ships departed. Nevertheless, by March 31 the fleet had covered only twenty leagues. Moreover, the Muslim pilot da Gama had arranged to take tried to trick him by presenting some islands sighted near dusk on that day as the mainland. The Captain-major had the pilot flogged for this offense and then named one of these islands the "island of the flogged one." After failing to find the "Christian island" described to him on Mozambique Island, da Gama decided to make for Mombasa on April 4. On April 6, the *São Rafael* ran aground on some shoals off Mtangata. While the Portuguese waited for high tide to free the ship, two Muslim craft approached the fleet "laden with fine oranges better than those in Portugal." Two of the African Muslims on these boats accompanied the fleet to Mombasa, which was reached the following day, Saturday, April 7, 1498.

Vasco da Gama and his men anchored off Mombasa with high expectations. Based on reports from the African Muslims now aboard the three ships: "we anchored here with much pleasure, for we confidently hoped that on the following day we might go on land and hear mass jointly with the Christians reported to live there under their own *alcaide* in a quarter separate from that of the Moors." The true state of affairs was soon revealed. The Muslims had "said this for a purpose of their own, for it was not true." Word of the arrival of these Christian ships had evidently spread quickly up the coast, and the Sultan of Mombasa had decided to disrupt this venture in any fashion possible. Given his experiences in Mozambique and distrust of his Muslim pilot, da Gama did not initially anchor in the port. An open Arab craft, or *zavra*, soon appeared loaded with men, who asked the Portuguese why they had come. Da Gama replied that he had come seeking provisions. Shrewd commander that he was, the Captain-major made sure that all of the sick were belowdecks and the remainder of the crews were fully armed on deck. Although these Muslim envoys promised assistance, da Gama set an all-night watch. At midnight, a *zavra* with 100 armed soldiers approached the *São Gabriel*. Da Gama only allowed four or five of these men aboard to parley, and it was obvious that "they paid us a visit merely to find out whether they might not capture one or the other of our vessels."

On Palm Sunday, April 8, the Sultan continued his ruse. He sent "two men, almost white, who said they were Christians, which appeared to be the fact" with gifts for da Gama. These men delivered "a sheep and large quantities of oranges, lemons, and sugar-cane, together with a ring as a pledge of safety, letting him know that in case of his entering the port he would be supplied with all he stood in need of." Da Gama sent back as a gift a string of coral pearls, delivered by two of the *degredados*. It is not exactly clear why da Gama responded in this fashion. Perhaps he hoped to insult the Sultan into revealing his true intentions, believing that if an open breech occurred, the lost of a string of beads and two convicts was better than a more elaborate gift delivered by one of his officers. In any case, the Sultan did not take the bait. The convicts were honorably received; allowed to stop at the house of two "Christian" merchants, who showed them "a sketch of the Holy Ghost," most probably a Hindu deity; and returned with samples of cloves and pepper.

On April 10, the Portuguese ships entered the port. A chance collision between the *São Gabriel* and one of the other ships created sufficient confusion for several of the African Muslims aboard to escape. This action prompted da Gama into more forceful measures in an effort to discover the true intentions of the Sultan. He had two of the remaining Muslims captured in Mozambique brought before him. He forcefully asked what they knew of the plot against the Portuguese. After they denied any knowledge, he tortured them using "the drops." Boiling oil was dripped onto their bare skin. "They said that orders had been given to capture us as soon as we entered the port, and thus to avenge what had been done at Mocambique." That night about midnight, two boats loaded with armed men approached the three ships. Some of these men entered the water, started to cut the cable of the *Berrio*, and had gotten hold of the rigging of the mizzenmast before they were discovered. The alarm was sounded and the attackers fled. As the *Roteiro* related, in a passage indicative of the nature of the Christian–Muslim conflict of this period: "These and other wicked tricks were practiced upon us by these dogs, but our Lord did not allow them to succeed, because they were unbelievers." Perhaps the best news for the fleet in Mombasa was that nearly all of the sick, many with scurvy, improved. "It pleased God in his mercy that on arriving at this city all our sick recovered their health, for the climate of this place is very good." Certainly the large quantities of oranges da Gama received had a good deal more to do with this miraculous recovery than the climate of the place. "After the malice and treachery planned by these dogs had been discovered, we still remained on Wednesday and Thursday [April 11–12]." Finally on the morning of April 13, the fleet departed and headed north once again. Upon crossing the bar, one of the ships, most likely the *Berrio*, lost an anchor. The Sultan had it raised and proudly displayed it near the town's gate until 1505, when Francisco de Almeida conquered Mombasa.

Da Gama still needed to arrange for an Arab or Indian pilot. The next morning two boats were sighted. The Portuguese ships gave chase "with the intention of capturing them, for we wanted to secure a pilot who would guide us to where we wanted to go." They managed to capture one loaded with seventeen men, gold, silver, provisions, and a "young woman, who was the wife of an old Moor of distinction . . . all threw themselves in the water, but we picked them up from our boats." On Saturday, April 14, 1498, the *São Gabriel*, *São Rafael*, and *Berrio* dropped anchor off the town of Malindi.

Having failed in an attempt to find an ally and a reliable pilot in both Mozambique and Mombasa, da Gama would at last find both in Malindi. Ironically, his ally would come in the form of another Muslim power, the Sultan of Malindi, a great rival of his Islamic colleague in Mombasa. The Sultan of Malindi evidently wanted a strong ally in his struggles along the East African coast, particularly against the powerful sultanate of Kilwa. Having heard of the exploits of this Christian fleet, he thought he had found such a power. On Easter Sunday, April 15, da Gama learned of four vessels belonging to "Christians" from India at anchor in the roadstead. The next day, the Captain-major landed the "old Moor of distinction" to act as his ambassador. That night, his envoy returned with an envoy from the Sultan, bearing a present of three sheep and an offer of friendship, provisions, and a pilot. At last sensing an ally, da Gama sent the Sultan an ecclesiastical cloak worn by the Brothers of Mercy in Portugal, two strings of coral, three washbasins, a hat, little bells, and two pieces of stripped *lambel* [stripped cotton cloth]. On April 17, the sultan sent da Gama six sheep, and "much cloves, cumin, nutmeg, and pepper." The sultan was elderly, and his son, acting as regent, came out on April 18 to negotiate with da Gama for some time. The next week was spent in friendly visits and festivities. Da Gama, although he released his Muslim prisoners as a sign of goodwill, remained wary in Malindi and never allowed his men ashore except in heavily armed boats. The Captain-major never landed, despite many entreaties and assurances.

During their stay in Malindi, the "Christian" captains of the four richly laden Indian ships visited the Portuguese fleet. Both Vasco and Paulo da Gama were present when these "Christians" first came aboard the *São Rafael*. There, they were shown "an altar-piece representing Our Lady at the foot of the cross, with Jesus Christ in her arms and the apostles around her." When the Indians saw this image, "they prostrated themselves, and as long as we were there they came to say their prayers in front of it, bringing offerings of cloves, pepper, and other things." Although these Hindus had obviously mistaken this image for one of their own deities, the fact remains that the episode reinforced da Gama's view, originally formed on Mozambique island, of them as "Christians." This opinion may have been further entrenched by an episode on April 19. On that day, Vasco da Gama and Nicolau Coelho reconnoitered the town from a longboat. As they passed the Indian ships, "these Indian Christians fired off many bombards from their vessels, and when they saw him pass they raised their hands and shouted lustily 'Christ! Christ!'" That night a feast was held by the Indians for the Portuguese at which "they warned the Captain-major against going on shore, and told him not to trust their 'fanfares' as they neither came from their hearts nor from their good will." According to the *Roteiro*: "These Indians are tawny men; they wear but little clothing and have long beards and long hair, which they braid. They told us they eat no beef. Their language differs from that of the Arabs, but some of them know a little of it, as they hold much intercourse with them."

Whether or not the Sultan could be trusted, he had most certainly failed to live up to his commitment to provide a pilot for da Gama. Accordingly, on April 22, when a boat appeared with an envoy from the Sultan, the Captain-major held him hostage. He then "sent word to the king that he required the pilots whom he had promised." Not long after, the Sultan indeed sent out a qualified pilot for the Portuguese fleet. According to the *Roteiro*, he sent "a Christian pilot" and da Gama was "much pleased" with this man. The exact identity of this pilot has been the subject of much speculation. The contemporary chroniclers called him "Malemo Cana" or "Malemo Canaca." For many years, historians believed he was one of the most famous Muslim navigators of the period, Ahmad ibn Majid. But this view has recently been undermined. All we can say with certainty is that the pilot was well trained and competent, and had made the voyage between East Africa to western India many times. He was in all probability a Muslim from Gujarat in India. But it is possible that, interpreting the lexicon of the *Roteiro*, he may indeed have been a "Christian," that is to say, a Hindu from Gujarat as well.

After spending nine days at Malindi, Vasco da Gama and his ships finally departed on April 24, 1498, for the main objective of his voyage: India. The fleet had been away from Lisbon for more than nine months. Dias's ships had demonstrated their seaworthiness on the difficult passage in the South Atlantic and in the currents along the east African coast. On the passage, Da Gama had demonstrated himself to be a master seaman, a competent warrior, and a ruthless enemy during the initial stage of the voyage. The Portuguese, quickly exposed as infidels, had also managed to traverse a hostile coast dominated by the "enemies" of Christian Europe. In doing so, da Gama had shown the superiority of European seaborne artillery and firepower, at least along the African littoral. Would the same advantage hold once India was reached? Da Gama had also learned that the adage "the enemy of my enemy is my friend" held true outside of Europe. Could this strategy be used to his advantage in India as well? He had a competent indigenous pilot to navigate the last maritime obstacle on the route to India. In short, the long preliminaries were over; the quest for the ultimate prize was ready to begin in earnest.

III

The Epic First Voyage: India and the Return Home, 1498–1499

*"May the Devil take thee! What brought you hither? . . .
And he told them that we came in search of Christians and
of spices." Roteiro from da Gama's First Voyage*

Summary

The chapter details Vasco da Gama's arrival on the pepper-rich Malabar coast of India in May 1498. Initial Portuguese perceptions and descriptions of Indian religious and social practices are examined, as are da Gama's attempts to negotiate for trading privileges in Calicut with the powerful Hindu ruler of that town. The quest of the Portuguese to overcome entrenched Arab opposition to their entrance into the lucrative pepper trade is described. The chapter concludes with the difficult return voyage of da Gama and his remaining ships to Lisbon.

Traversing the Arabian Sea and Arrival in India

The Gujarati pilot that da Gama arranged in Malindi, whether Muslim or Hindu, was competent, and the voyage across the Arabian Sea to India was uneventful and successful. On April 29, the Portuguese happily "once more saw the North Star, which we had not seen for a long time." The passage took twenty-three days and, according to the *Roteiro*, "we could not have made less than 600 leagues." On May 18, lofty mountains, including Mount Eli in northern Kerala, were sighted. The monsoon rains had already begun on the western coast of India, and adverse weather forced the fleet to sail offshore until Sunday, May 20, 1498. The weather cleared and the pilot recognized the fleet's location. He informed Vasco da Gama that they "were above Calecut that this was the country we desired to go." By nightfall, the *São Gabriel*, the *São Rafael*, and the *Berrio* anchored just north of Calicut between that city and the village of Pantalayini-Kollam, or Pandarane. After nearly eleven months of sailing, traversing thousands of miles of ocean, and overcoming both sickness and hostile powers along the African coast, da Gama had reached the ultimate goal of Prince Henry and D. João II. The sea route to India had at last been achieved. D. Manuel I had placed great confidence in him, and da Gama had more than justified his selection to command the expedition. Nevertheless, as soon as the Malabar Coast had been reached, the next question in the progression of challenges confronting da Gama loomed: What type of reception would the Portuguese receive in India?

The Political, Economic, and Social Situation in Calicut

The pepper-rich Malabar coast of India extends for roughly 150 miles, from Mount Eli in the north to Cape Comorin in the south. This fertile coast is separated from the rest of the Indian subcontinent by a range of hills called the Western Ghats. At the time of da Gama's arrival, the geopolitical situation there was similar to that on the east coast of Africa. A host of rival small states existed, and these kingdoms were engaged in a fierce struggle for economic and political power, a struggle that was intimately tied to the rich trade in spices, especially pepper, based in the region. In 1498, Calicut was the most important of these states. It was strategically located not only with respect to pepper production, but also with respect to the trading routes

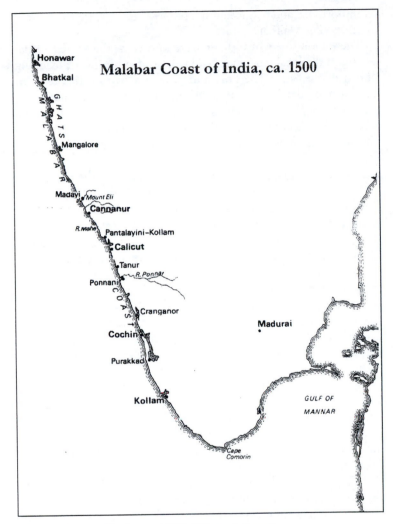

Malabar Coast of India, ca. 1500. (Glenn J. Ames)

that had been established by the Arabs in the preceding centuries. These routes linked east Africa, India, Persia, Arabia, the
Red Sea ports, Melaka, China, and Indonesia. Da Gama knew

its importance and had asked his pilot to set a course for Calicut upon leaving Malindi.

The Hindu rulers of Calicut were known as the *Samudri raja*, a term in the local language, Malayalam, from Sanskrit meaning "Lord of the Sea." The Portuguese would corrupt this term to Zamorin or Samorin. Unlike in Europe, the royal succession passed through the female line, with the first son born to the king's eldest sister the heir to the throne. The Hindu social hierarchy was dominated by two castes: the Brahmins dominated the religious and intellectual life of the city, while the warrior Nairs dominated the military and bolstered the power of the Samudri.

Calicut, however, did not possess a fine harbor. To compensate for this disadvantage, successive Zamorins had done their utmost to attract trade through a variety of strategies. Relatively low customs duties, freedom of religion, the building of a large navy, and giving favor to the Nairs had all assisted the rise of Calicut to the greatest transport center on the Malabar coast. In the bustling markets of the town, Gujaratis, Persians, Syrians, Turks, Somalis, Chinese, Malays, Nestorian Christians, and Jews all traded under the auspices of the Zamorin. Yet, the most favored and powerful group was the Muslim community, made up of foreign Arab traders resident in the city as well as local Kerala Muslims called **Mappilas**.

By the late fifteenth century, Islam had spread throughout the Indian Ocean basin, and this religious diaspora had been accompanied by the spread of Muslim mercantile power as well. Arabs dominated the seaborne trade along the Indian coast; and Arabs, along with the Mappilas, dominated the trade of Calicut. The Muslim community had invested much time and many gifts to the Zamorin to achieve this favored position. The Arabs had their own quarter of the city for warehouses and shops, as well as their own judges and religious leaders. They were even allowed to encourage conversion to Islam without interference. Dwelling in the Arab quarter were the so-called Moplahs, individuals who had an Arab father and an Indian mother. Given the ongoing religious struggle in Europe and the Near East, the Muslim lobby in Calicut certainly had the most to lose from the appearance of a Christian power in India. They were determined to do everything they could to prevent da Gama from cultivating an alliance with the Zamorin and winning the spoils of the rich pepper trade. Word of da Gama's rather checkered experiences on the east coast of Africa had reached Calicut in advance of his arrival through Muslim merchants plying the trade, thus warning of the approach of these Christians.

Initial Contacts with the "Christians" and Muslims of Calicut

Soon after anchoring, four small boats loaded with men approached the Portuguese ships. Speaking in Arabic, they made inquiries regarding the origin of the fleet. The next day, these same boats reappeared. Da Gama had ordered João Nunes, the convict-exile and converted Jew who spoke some Arabic and Hebrew, to accompany these men to shore to reconnoiter the place. Upon landing, Nunes was taken to the house of two Arabs from Tunis, including one referred to as Monçaide (*el Masud*, the happy one?). This action may have been taken because the Portuguese, as in Mombasa, had been mistaken for Muslims from the Near East or North Africa. Nunes was also taken to these Muslims for a more practical reason; they "could speak Castilian and Genoese." It is significant that at this momentous occasion of the first contact between West and East via the Cape route the interchange for the Portuguese took place with these Castilian-speaking Muslims, not Indians. These Muslims embodied the entrenched power that Islam enjoyed in the Indian Ocean trade. They represented the traditional trading system linking the Mediterranean and Indian Ocean that had helped to make Islam and, by extension, Catholic Italian city-states like Venice, so powerful during the fifteenth century. This power had been demonstrated first in Mehmet II's conquest of Constantinople, the bastion of eastern Christianity, in 1453 on the one hand, and the glories of the Italian Renaissance on the other.

Da Gama's discovery of the sea route to the Indian Ocean via the Cape of Good Hope embodied a direct challenge to that system by outflanking the traditional trading routes through the

Near East. Perhaps recognizing this implicit threat, the "first greeting that he [Nunes] received was in these words: 'May the Devil take thee! What brought you hither?'" According to the *Roteiro*, Monçaide and his friend then asked what the Portuguese sought so far from home. Nunes replied that they had come "in search of Christians and of spices." Monçaide asked why the kings of Castile, or France, or the rulers of Venice had not sent ships. Nunes replied, "Because the king of Portugal will not permit it." After being given wheat bread and honey, Nunes returned back to the *São Gabriel* with Monçaide.

When Monçaide met da Gama aboard the flagship, he exclaimed: "A lucky venture! A lucky venture! Plenty of rubies, plenty of emeralds! You owe great thanks for God, for having brought you to country holding such riches." As the author of the *Roteiro* noted, "We were greatly astonished to hear this talk, for we never expected to hear our language spoken so far away from Portugal." For his part, da Gama must have been convinced that he had indeed made a wise choice in heading for Calicut. The problem was how to obtain this wealth, especially as it must have been obvious from these early encounters that the Muslims controlled the trade all along the Indian coast. The Zamorin was the key to the entire situation; win him over and everything else was possible, Muslims or no Muslims. Monçaide informed the Portuguese that the Zamorin was then at the town of Ponnani, some twenty-eight miles south of Calicut.

The Captain-major sent Fernão Martins to Ponnani with the accommodating Monçaide to announce to the Zamorin that an ambassador from the king of Portugal had arrived with formal letters. Martins bore instructions to tell the local ruler that, if necessary, these letters could be sent to Ponnani. The Portuguese envoys, however, were graciously received by the Zamorin, who informed them that he was returning to Calicut. He presented the "bearers of this message with much fine cloth." The Zamorin also sent one of his pilots, who conducted the Portuguese ships to a better anchorage off Pantalayini, a little north of the city. Da Gama, however, wary after events on the African coast, refused to "anchor as near the shore as the king's pilot desired." A message and delegation from the Zamorin soon arrived, inviting da Gama to a formal interview. This delegation included a *bale* (*wali* in Arabic=governor) "like an *alcaide*" who was "always attended by two hundred men armed with swords and bucklers." Because it was almost nightfall, da Gama delayed the meeting until the following day.

Da Gama's First Audience with the Zamorin of Calicut

On the morning of May 28, 1498, Vasco da Gama and thirteen of his men, including the author of the *Roteiro*, set out for their historic meeting with the Zamorin. Despite the toll of the long voyage, da Gama sought to impress his host: "we put on our best attire, placed bombards in our boats, and took with us trumpets and many flags." Paulo da Gama was left in command of the three ships, while Nicolau Coelho was ordered to wait by the ship's boats until the Captain-major and his men returned. Once on shore, the Portuguese were met by the *alcaide* "with whom were many men, armed and unarmed." Da Gama was allowed to ride in a palanquin, or covered litter carried by shifts of six men, while his men walked. "The reception was friendly, as if the people were pleased to see us." At the village of Kappatt, the Portuguese were given a meal of fish and heavily buttered rice. Da Gama, however, either out of distaste, anxiety, or suspicion, did not eat.

At Kappatt, the Portuguese entered boats on the Elatur River to cover the remaining seven miles to Calicut. "There were numerous other boats, all crowded with people. As to those who were on the banks I say nothing; their number was infinite, and they had all come to see us." Upon disembarking from these ferries, da Gama again entered his palanquin. The Portuguese finally entered Calicut; "the road was crowded with a countless multitude anxious to see us. Even the women came out of their houses with children in their arms and followed us." In a region accustomed to welcoming traders from throughout the Indian Ocean basin, this rather frenzied reception suggests that the Portuguese had already been identified as different. News of their escapades on the east coast of Africa had already reached the Malabar coast. These Christians had now appeared and were on their way to meet with the Zamorin. The local populace clearly wanted to know what they looked like.

Upon entering the city, da Gama and his men were taken to a Hindu Vaishnava temple. Da Gama and most of his crew still believed that the Indians were "Christians." Indeed, the author of the *Roteiro* began this section of his journal: "The city of Calecut is inhabited by Christians." It is hardly surprising, therefore, that da Gama and his men sought to describe and interpret what they saw in this temple entirely within the model of Christianity. "The body of the church is as large as a monastery . . . in the center of the body of the church rose a chapel . . . within this sanctuary stood a small image which they said represented Our Lady." As they were not Brahmins, the Portuguese were not allowed into this inner sanctum. But according to one source, the priests crowded around them, pointing at this statue, crying, "Maria, Maria." This statue probably depicted the local deity Mari or Mariamma, the much-feared goddess of smallpox.

One aspect of this first encounter between the Portuguese and Indians that should be constantly kept in mind is the language barrier and *ad hoc* means of communication that existed between the two cultures. Because none of the Portuguese spoke the local language of Malayalam, da Gama communicated in Arabic, utilizing the skills of Fernão Martins. But Martins had learned his Arabic in North Africa, and there were subtle differences in the dialect spoken along the Indian coast. In any event, these Brahmin priests called "*quafees* (Arabic terms *qasîs* and *kâfir*=unbelievers) threw holy water over us, and gave us some white earth which the Christians of this country are in the habit of putting on their foreheads, breasts, around the neck, and on the forearms." Vasco da Gama refused to put this mixture of dust, cow dung, sacrificial ashes, and sandalwood mixed with rice water on his body, but gave it to one of his men saying "he would put it on later." "Many other saints were painted on the walls of the church, wearing crowns . . . with teeth protruding an inch from the mouth, and four or five arms." "In this church the captain-major said his prayers, and we with him." Even at this point, however, not everyone believed that the Hindus were members of an eastern Christian sect. According to the chronicler Castanheda, while praying, João de Sá knelt next to Vasco da Gama and whispered: "If these be devils, I worship the true God." Da Gama gave him one of his rare smiles.

By the time the delegation reached the Zamorin's palace, the crowd grew so thick that progress along the street became next to impossible. The whole day had also been consumed, and the sun was setting. The Zamorin received da Gama and his men in a small courtyard. The Portuguese were obviously impressed by the signs of wealth surrounding his person and court. "The king was in a small court, reclining upon a couch covered with a cloth of green velvet . . . in his left hand [he] held a very large golden cup [spittoon] having a capacity of half an *almude* [eight pints] . . . on the right side of the king stood a basin of gold, so large that a man might just encircle it with his arms." The Zamorin, on an admittedly grand scale, was indulging in the Indian passion of chewing and spitting betel nut. Da Gama entered and "saluted in the manner of the country: by putting the hands together, then raising them toward Heaven, as is done by Christians when addressing God." The Zamorin beckoned the Portuguese to sit on a stone bench where he could see them. He then ordered that water for their hands should be provided and that bananas and jack fruit be served.

Through an Arabic-speaking interpreter, the Zamorin asked da Gama to tell him of his voyage and its purpose. The *Capitão-mor* stated that he was an ambassador of the King of Portugal and the bearer of a message that he could only deliver to him personally. The Zamorin said this was acceptable, and da Gama, accompanied by Fernão Martins, entered a more private room. The local ruler then joined da Gama, accompanied, according to Góis, by his Brahmin chief minister, his betel carrier, and his factor or business agent. "The king, when he joined the captain, threw himself upon another couch, covered with various stuffs embroidered in gold, and asked the captain what he wanted."

Da Gama, through his interpreter, described the King of Portugal "who was Lord of many countries and the possessor of great wealth of every description, exceeding that of any king of these parts." He recounted the long history of sixty years of voyages under Prince Henry and D. João II, which had culminated in this expedition. Believing that the Zamorin was Christian, and wishing to forge a solid link with him while distancing himself from the Muslims who controlled the trade, da Gama stressed the religious component of the voyage, not the economic. The Portuguese had sought to make discoveries in the direction of India, as they knew that there were Christian kings there like themselves. This was the reason that induced them to seek this country, not because they sought gold or silver, for this "they had such abundance that they needed not what was to be found in this country." D. Manuel had ordered him "not to return to Portugal until he should have discovered this King of the Christians, on pain of having his head cut off."

According to the chronicler Osório, da Gama concluded by stating that his king "having heard much of India, particularly of the empire of Calicut . . . as well as the dignity and grandeur of their sovereign" was extremely anxious to enter into a league of friendship with so renowned a monarch. The Captain-major stressed the mutual advantages of such a league. He concluded by announcing he carried two letters to be presented when he reached India. The Zamorin replied that the Portuguese were welcome, and that, "on his part, he held him [D. Manuel] as a friend and brother." Da Gama had earlier stated that he could not present himself "before his king and master unless he was able to present, at the same time, some men of this country." The Zamorin agreed to send ambassadors to Portugal. As it was already 10 o'clock at night, the audience concluded. The local ruler asked if the Portuguese wished to lodge with "Christians" or Muslims. Da Gama replied "neither"; "and begged as a favor that he be given a lodging by himself." He then left in his palanquin, followed by his men and a throng of Indians.

Tensions Between the Portuguese and Muslims in Calicut

Beginning the next morning, May 29, the promising beginning to da Gama's quest for an alliance with the Zamorin began to deteriorate. There has been much debate on the strained relationship that soon developed between the Portuguese and the ruler of Calicut. One view argues that whatever intentions the Zamorin held toward allying with the Portuguese were undermined by the money and influence of the jealous Muslim community in Calicut. An opposing view holds that da Gama's heavy-handed diplomacy and temper undermined any chance for an alliance and that the Zamorin acted with fairness and honor from the end of May through da Gama's departure in August. A compromise approach provides the best explanation for the events of these months. The entrenched Muslim community in Calicut certainly viewed da Gama and his men as Christian shock troops of the continuing crusade in Europe and the Near East and did everything in its power to undermine Portuguese diplomacy. Initially, the Zamorin may have been willing to consider the Portuguese as a welcome counterweight to the Muslims. Yet any plans for an economic accommodation that would increase his wealth through rising competition for pepper was subverted by the hatred that existed between the two religions at this time. The Zamorin came to realize that he would have to embrace one set of foreigners or the other. As for da Gama, he generally conducted himself with prudence and restraint in an effort to achieve an alliance or, failing that, at least a rich cargo of spices for the return to Lisbon.

Da Gama's Presents for the Zamorin and a Second Audience

Problems began when da Gama prepared his gifts for the Zamorin. These included "twelve pieces of striped cloth, four scarlet hoods, six hats, four strings of coral, a case containing six wash-hand basins, a case of sugar, two casks of oil, and two of honey." As it was "the custom not to send anything to the king without the knowledge of the Moor, his factor, and of the *bale*" da Gama summoned these officials to inspect his gifts. Upon seeing these gifts, these men "laughed at it, saying that it was not a thing to offer to a king, that the poorest merchant from Mecca, or any other part of India, gave more." They told the Captain-major that if he wanted to make a present it should be in gold, as the king would not accept such things. While da Gama probably realized the truth of these statements, he had no other choice, since he had no gold. He adopted perhaps the only line of defense he could, declaring that he was not "a merchant, but an ambassador; that he gave of that which he had, which was his own and not the king's." If D. Manuel ordered his return, he would entrust him with far richer presents. It was a nice effort, but the Zamorin's envoys flatly refused to forward them or to allow da Gama to send them on his own. After they had departed, other Muslim merchants appeared, and they all depreciated da Gama's presents. Obviously, if these were the only gifts the Portuguese possessed, Muslim predominance in the trading network was not in jeopardy.

At this point, da Gama requested a second audience with the Zamorin. The factor and *bale* told him that if he would wait a short time, they would return and accompany him to the palace. But they did not return that day. "The captain was very wroth at being among so phlegmatic and unreliable a people," and considered going to the palace himself. In the end, da Gama decided it was best to wait until the following day. While he may have been in a foul mood for most of May 29, the rest of the delegation made the best of the situation: "we diverted ourselves, singing and dancing to the sound of trumpets, and enjoyed ourselves much."

On May 30, a second audience did take place with the Zamorin. This time, the palace was crowded with armed men. Da Gama was kept waiting for four long hours outside a door. When finally admitted, the Captain-major was allowed to take only two men with him. The Zamorin was more curt and less gracious than at their first meeting. He informed da Gama that he had expected him the previous day. Instead of blaming the Zamorin's factor and *bale*, da Gama diplomatically stated that "the long road had tired him, and for that reason he had not come." The Zamorin then stated that although da Gama claimed to come from a very rich kingdom, he had brought him nothing. Moreover, he had not yet been delivered his letter. Da Gama stated that the object of his voyage was merely to make discoveries, but when other ships came, they would bring suitable presents. As for the letter, he promised to deliver it immediately.

Two factors were responsible for this shift in attitude on the part of the Zamorin: the truly paltry and inexcusable quality of the gifts da Gama carried and the lobbying of the Muslim community in Calicut. On the one hand, the Muslims pressed their role as dutiful and useful subjects who had done so much to facilitate the economic prosperity of the city. They implored the Zamorin not to allow this ancient friendship "to be dissolved by a set of abandoned wretches lately arrived in these parts." The Muslims also emphasized the warlike nature of the Portuguese and strove to present da Gama to the Zamorin as "a cruel, bloody-minded pyrate" who would upset the prosperity that had benefited both the ruler and his loyal Muslim traders.

At this second audience, the Zamorin intimated that the golden image of a Santa Maria from the *São Gabriel* might soothe his feelings over the lack of suitable gifts. Da Gama, however, told him that this image was not made of gold, and "even if she were he would not part with her, as she had guided him across the ocean, and would guide him back to his own country." The Zamorin then pressed again for his formal letters from D. Manuel. The Captain-major carried two letters: one in Portuguese and one in Arabic. Because da Gama had already heard of the Muslim intrigues against him at court, he asked that a "Christian" who was able to speak Arabic be provided, since the "Moors wished him ill and might misinterpret him." A young man named Quaram was called, but he could only speak Arabic, not read it. Finally, four Muslims at court took the letter and "translated it to the king, who was well satisfied with its contents." The interview continued with a discussion of the trading products that were found in Portugal. Da Gama told the Zamorin that there was much corn, cloth, iron, bronze, and many other products and that he carried samples. The Captain-major added that "if permitted to return to the ships, he would order it to be landed, and that meantime four or five men would remain at the lodgings." But the Zamorin said no. "He might take all his people with him, securely moor his ships, land his merchandise, and sell it to the best advantage." On this rather abrupt note, the second and final audience between Vasco da Gama and the Zamorin ended.

Tensions Mount: A Disputed Return to the Ships

On May 31, 1498, da Gama and his men marched back to the anchorage off Pantalayini. On this journey the Captain-major outdistanced his men, who wandered inland. The Portuguese later reunited at a rest-house at Pantalayini, where travelers usually found protection against the monsoon rains. Da Gama then asked the *bale* for boats to take them back to their ships. As the hour was late, "in fact the sun had set," the *bale* refused and suggested the Portuguese stay ashore until the next day. Da Gama, however, threatened to return to the Zamorin to complain about this effort to detain him—"a very bad thing, as he was a Christian like themselves." This threat and the look on da Gama's face convinced the *bale* to reconsider, and he led the Portuguese along the beach, looking for boats for a time. On this trip, da Gama, who suspected "some evil design," sent three of his men out in advance to warn Paulo and Coelho. By the end of the night, da Gama and his remaining men returned to the house of a Muslim: "the captain ordered fowls and rice to be purchased, and we ate, notwithstanding our fatigue, having been all day on our legs."

The next morning, da Gama again asked for boats to conduct him to his ships. He was told that he if ordered his ships nearer the shore this request would be granted. Da Gama refused and again threatened to appeal directly to the Zamorin, "who was a Christian like himself." At that point, all the doors of the house were closed and an armed guard posted. None of the Portuguese could leave except under close guard. The *bale* then requested that the Portuguese "give up our sails and rudders," thus imprisoning the ships as well. At this crucial moment, da Gama demonstrated the qualities of leadership that D. Manuel believed he possessed. "The Captain declared that he would give up none of these things . . . they might do with him whatever they liked, but he would give up nothing." Da Gama then asked that he be held but that his men be allowed to return to the ships "as at the place they were in they would die of hunger." But the *bale* said that "if we died of hunger we must bear it, as they cared nothing for that." For the remainder of June 1, da Gama and the *bale* sparred over the issue of ordering the ships closer to shore. The Captain-major steadfastly refused, out of the belief that if he did so, the ships "could be easily captured, after which they would first kill him, and then us others, as we were already in their power." In fact, throughout that night they were guarded by "over a hundred men, all armed with swords, two-edged battle axes, shields, and bows and arrows."

This tense stalemate was broken the following day. The *bale*, perhaps after a conversation with the Zamorin, returned with his aides, all wearing "better faces." Based supposedly on local custom, he offered da Gama a deal: If he would land all of his merchandise and crews, and if the vendors would remain ashore until all of these goods were sold, then da Gama could return to his ships. Da Gama wrote to Paulo and ordered some goods sent to shore. As soon as these goods were landed, he and his men were allowed to return to their ships. Diogo Dias, as factor, and Alvaro de Braga, as his assistant, remained at Pantalayini to oversee the sale of these goods. "At this we rejoiced greatly, and rendered thanks to God for having extricated us from the hands of people who had no more sense than beasts, for we knew well that once the captain was on board those who had been landed would have nothing to fear."

Difficulties in Loading a Cargo, June–August 1498

As soon as Vasco da Gama reached the *São Gabriel*, he ordered that no more merchandise should be landed. For the next five days, the *bale* and Muslim merchants in town did everything they could to belittle these goods. Hindu merchants were also unimpressed. On June 7, da Gama wrote to the Zamorin to complain of his detention and these actions by the Muslims. The Zamorin sent a reply chastising these merchants as "bad Christians." He sent "seven or eight merchants to inspect the merchandise, and to become purchasers if they felt inclined." A "man of quality" was also dispatched to remain with "the factor already there, and authorized them to kill any Moor who might go there, without fear of punishment." While these steps give the impression of support from the Zamorin, nothing in fact changed with respect to selling the Portuguese wares. The Zamorin's merchants not only refused to buy; they, too, belittled the merchandise. The Muslim merchants avoided the Portuguese factory or warehouse but "when one of us landed they spat on the ground saying: 'Portugal, Portugal.' Indeed from the very first they had sought means to take and kill us."

On June 23, 1498, given the moribund nature of the trade at Pantalayini, da Gama successfully applied for permission from the Zamorin to move this merchandise to Calicut. Although his true motives toward the Portuguese are not clear, he at least gave the appearance of support. He ordered the *bale* to recruit sufficient men "to carry the whole on their backs to Calecut, this to be done at his own expense, as nothing belonging to the King of Portugal was to be burdened with expenses whilst in his country." In Calicut, Dias and de Braga did not have much more success. Nevertheless, from late June into early August the Portuguese tried to sell their wares. Da Gama, moreover, instituted a rotating shore leave for the crews of the ships so that each "would be able to make such purchases as they desired." The crew members were generally well treated by the Hindus. "These men were made welcome by the Christians along the road who showed much pleasure when one of them entered a house, to eat or sleep, and they gave them freely of all they had." During these months, da Gama welcomed any Hindus who could be ferried out to his ships; he traded with them and fed them. "All this was done for the sake of establishing relations of peace and amity, and to induce them to speak well of us and not evil."

Evidently this plan worked too well, as "so great was the number of these visitors that sometimes it was night before we could get rid of them." As the author of the *Roteiro* argued, these great numbers were due "to the dense population of the country and the scarcity of food." In this bartering, the Portuguese usually traded tin "bracelets, clothes, new shirts, and other articles which they desired to sell." At times, the prices for these some Portuguese goods were not what da Gama had hoped for: "a very fine shirt which in Portugal fetches 300 *reis*, was worth here only two *fanôes*, which is equivalent to only 30 *reis*." Clearly, European clothing would not export well to India. Yet, the Portuguese were able to obtain samples of the products they coveted for shipment to Europe: cloves, cinnamon, pepper, and precious stones. By early August, da Gama decided that nothing more could be accomplished, and he began to make preparations for his departure. One issue the Captain-major considered was whether to leave behind a permanent Portuguese presence, composed of Dias as factor, de Braga as his scribe-assistant, Fernão Martins, and perhaps four others. In return, however, he wanted to take local men back to Portugal, both as tangible proof he had reached India and as a counterbalance to the men he would leave in Calicut.

On August 9, Diogo Dias was sent to the Zamorin with gifts, including amber and coral. Dias also carried a message informing the ruler of da Gama's wish to depart and his offer to leave his factor and others behind provided local men were sent to Portugal. In return for the present, he requested "on behalf of his lord [D. Manuel] a *bahar* [=ca. 459 lbs.] of cinnamon, a *bahar* of cloves as also samples of such other spices as he thought proper, saying that the factor would pay for them, if he desired it." By this point, the Muslim lobby had been at work for some time with both verbal and monetary inducements for the Zamorin. Predictably, Dias received a less than cordial reception. He was kept waiting for four days before he was received, and then with very little ceremony. At this audience, the Zamorin told Dias that he should have given the present to his Muslim factor and that he did not want to look at it. He was also instructed to inform da Gama that before he could leave he had to pay some 600 *xerafins* in duties; "this was the custom of the country and of those who came to it." Dias was followed from the palace back to the house the Portuguese were using to store their products; these guards sequestered the goods, and a proclamation was issued forbidding any more boats from approaching the Portuguese ships. Dias, using an Indian boy as messenger, managed to smuggle out his report to da Gama.

As the author of the *Roteiro* noted, "this news made us sad; not only because we saw some of our men in the hands of our enemies but also because it interfered with our departure." Did the Zamorin simply want his customs duties and held Dias and his men as collateral to receive them? It appears that there was a good deal more afoot than customs duties. According to Monçaide, the Muslims of Calicut "who were merchants from Mecca and elsewhere, and who knew us, could ill digest us. They had told the king that we were thieves, and that if once we navigated to his country, no more ships from Mecca, nor from Quambaye [Gujarat], nor from Imgros [Hurmuz?], nor from any other part, would visit him." Large bribes had been offered to the Zamorin "to capture and kill us, so that we should not return to Portugal . . . if the captains went ashore their heads would be cut off." Given the contemporary hatred between the Portuguese and Muslims, the Zamorin had been forced to choose between these enemies. By mid-August 1498, he had embraced the rich foreigners who had done much for his kingdom as opposed to the hundred or so men on three strange ships, with pitiful presents to offer and a history and religion he knew little about. At the time, it seemed like a wise choice.

Nevertheless, the one thing that had already saved da Gama and the Portuguese several times on this voyage would do so again at Calicut: the superiority of their ships and especially the artillery they carried. As long as the Captain-major and his men remained anchored offshore aboard ship, they were untouchable. The main problem for da Gama was how to regain Dias and the other hostages. In this matter, his ruthless skills of command were again displayed to great effect. Beginning on August 15, da Gama welcomed people aboard his ships for bartering. "When the people saw that no harm befell them, there came daily many merchants, and other who were not merchants, from curiousity, and all were made welcome by us and given [things] to eat." On Sunday, August 19, twenty-five men came aboard, including "six persons of quality." Da Gama "perceived that through these we might recover the men who were detained as prisoners on land." He, therefore, held these six and an additional twelve men as prisoners to trade for his own men. The rest of these visitors were put on a ship's boat and sent to shore with a message for the Zamorin's Muslim factor: Release the Portuguese prisoners and goods and these men would be returned.

The Decision to Return to Portugal

The next few days brought no response. Therefore, on August 23, da Gama ordered his ships to weigh anchor and set sail. The Captain-major sent word to shore that he was returning to

Portugal but that he hoped to return soon "and that then they would know whether we were robbers." Contrary headwinds, however, prevented the Portuguese from leaving the coast. Three days later, they were still anchored within sight of Calicut. A boat approached, bearing a message from the Zamorin telling da Gama that Dias was in the royal palace and that if the hostages were freed, he would be brought to the Portuguese fleet. The Captain-major, however, understandably suspected a trick: He "was of the opinion that he [Dias] had been killed, and that they said this in order to detain us until they had completed their armaments, or until ships of Mecca able to capture us had arrived." Accordingly, da Gama gave these envoys an ultimatum: Leave at once or he would fire his bombards on them.

Before departing, these envoys were told to deliver Dias, his men, or a letter from them proving they were still alive or da Gama would behead all of his captives. This bold move had the desired effect. The Zamorin called Diogo Dias before him and "received him with marked kindness." In their conversation, he denied any knowledge of his detainment or the demand for 600 *xerafins* and told him that "the factor alone was responsible for this extortion." The Zamorin even rebuked his Muslim factor in front of Dias, asking him whether he knew that "quite recently he had killed another factor because he had levied tribute upon some merchants that had come" to Calicut. He told Dias that he could go to the *São Gabriel* and arrange the return of the hostages held by da Gama. In return, the Zamorin would erect a *padrão* in the city and allow Dias to remain and trade his merchandise. He then requested that Dias write a letter for his king, D. Manuel. In this letter, the Zamorin acknowledged that Vasco da Gama, "a gentleman of your household came to my country, whereat I was pleased." Further, he informed D. Manuel that his country was rich "in cinnamon, ginger, pepper, and precious stones." In exchange, the Zamorin asked for "gold, silver, corals and scarlet cloth."

On the morning of the August 27, seven boats approached the *São Gabriel*. Believing that Dias would return to Calicut with them, the Zamorin's men had not embarked da Gama's trading goods. Fearing the Captain-major's wrath, Dias and the others were deposited in the ship's longboat, which was roped to the stern of the flagship. Dias then delivered the Zamorin's message regarding the hostages, the *padrão*, and the request to remain as a factor in Calicut. Da Gama provided the *padrão* and released his six most distinguished prisoners, promising to turn over the rest when his goods were returned. Yet he would not allow Dias to return to shore. Early the next day, Monçaide appeared. He told da Gama that "all he had had been taken from him, that worse might happen, and that this was his usual luck." The "people of the country" had charged him with "being a Christian, who had come to Calecut by order of the King of Portugal; for this reason he preferred going away with us rather than remain in a country where any day he might be killed." Da Gama agreed to this request. Soon thereafter, three more boats approached the *São Gabriel* carrying some striped cloth.

An envoy told the Portuguese that "this was all the merchandise which belonged us." In fact, it was only a portion of the goods onshore. These men offered a simple deal: Turn over the remaining hostages first, and the cloth would be returned. Da Gama, however, "saw through their cunning, and the Captain-major told them to go away, saying he cared nought for the merchandise, but wanted to take these men to Portugal." In order to prove his discoveries to D. Manuel, da Gama badly needed to return with inhabitants of India. From his arrival, his plans included arranging such authentication either peacefully or by force. Accordingly, the lure of regaining his merchandise paled in comparison to the value of a return cargo of Indians. Da Gama also told these men that he would shortly return to Calicut and at that time "they would know whether we were thieves, as had been told them by the Moors."

On Wednesday, August 29, 1498, the Captain-major held a council with his officers. They decided that because they had "discovered the country we came in search of, as also spices and precious stones, and it appeared impossible to establish cordial relations with the people, it would be as well to take our departure." The flags were unfurled, a few rounds of cannon were fired, and after approximately three months at Calicut, the Portuguese fleet departed.

The Return Voyage: August 1498– September 1499

The voyage home would teach da Gama several valuable lessons. One of these lessons was that neither the Muslim traders who controlled the trade in the Indian Ocean nor their indigenous allies were going to allow the Portuguese to break into this trade peacefully. This point, originally made in Calicut, was reiterated on August 30. The fleet was becalmed about a league north of the city when "about seventy boats filled with armed men approached." Da Gama waited for them to approach within range of the bombards and then "ordered us to fire upon them." As the wind freshened, the Portuguese ships made way, but these boats followed for an hour and a half, until a thunderstorm broke. At that point, according to the author of the *Roteiro*, the Portuguese were "carried out to sea; and when they saw they could no longer do us harm they turned back, whilst we pursued our route." This route carried da Gama and his ships north along the coast. On September 10, near Cannanur, whose king, Biaquotte [sic], was at war with the King of Calicut, the Captain-major landed one of his six hostages "who had lost an eye." He carried a letter in Arabic written by Monçaide for the Zamorin. Da Gama made three main points. He stated that he had only taken the hostages with him so that they might bear witness to his great discoveries. He claimed that he would have left Dias as a factor but had not done so out of a fear the Muslims would kill him. He also expressed a desire for friendly relations with the Zamorin in the future. Five days later, a *padrão* was erected on one of the Netrani islands. At this point, Vasco da Gama realized that before traversing the Arabian Sea on the way to Africa, the ships would have to be careened. With this necessity in mind, the fleet anchored at the Anjedive Islands on September 20.

The fleet remained at this group of six islands located south of Goa for nearly two weeks. During this stay, the ships were cleaned and wood, water, and vegetables taken on. Da Gama also arranged for some samples of cinnamon to bring back to Lisbon. On the morning of September 22, two fairly large ships appeared, followed by six others. Da Gama "at once gave orders to sink these vessels." In the engagement that ensued, seven of these ships grounded themselves to avoid capture and were fired upon by the Portuguese. The other ship was disabled, her crew fled, and the Portuguese captured her. As the author of the *Roteiro* noted with disappointment on this prize: "we . . . found nothing in her except provisions, coco-nuts, four jars of palm-sugar, and arms, all the rest being sand used as ballast." The next day, a boat approached the Portuguese anchorage and the men aboard told da Gama that the seven ships "had come from Calecut in search of us [the Portuguese], and that if they had succeeded in taking us we should have been killed." Da Gama encountered more unwelcome visitors on September 24. Anchored off the largest island in the group, the *Berrio* and *São Gabriel* were careened on the beach when two large boats crowded with people and rowing "to the sound of drums and bagpipes, and displayed flags at the masthead" approached. "Five other boats remained on the coast for their protection." Da Gama's hostages told him that these boats were pirates who would seize them if they could. Although he was in a somewhat vulnerable position, the Captain-major not only ordered the *São Rafael* to fire on these ships, but also managed to fire off rounds from his own ship as well. Under the fury of this bombardment, the ships fled. These vessels probably belonged to the Hindu "pirate" **Timoja**, who was based at nearby Honawar and would later assist the Portuguese. What is certain is that the shipborne artillery of the Portuguese had once again saved them, a lesson that clearly was not lost on da Gama.

While anchored at the Anjedive islands, a man appeared who would play a notable role in the subsequent Portuguese presence in India. He was "about forty years of age," spoke "Venetian" well, and was wearing a "fine hat on his head and a sword in his belt." This man told da Gama that he was a Christian who had come to India from the west early in his youth. He was now serving the Muslim ruler of the rich city of Goa, "who could muster 40,000 horsemen." Although he had converted to Islam, this man told the Portuguese he was "at heart still a Christian." When news had reached Goa that "Franks" had reached Calicut, "whose speech none could understand," he had "begged permission of his master to be allowed to visit." His lord had agreed, with the message that the Portuguese could have anything they needed and that if they "decided to remain permanently it would give him much pleasure." Da Gama thanked this visitor for his offer and gave him cheese and bread. Yet the man was not content and kept "talking so much about so many things, that at times he contradicted himself."

No doubt suspicious, Paulo da Gama asked the Hindus who accompanied this man who he was; the reply was that he was a "pirate" who had come to attack the Portuguese. Vasco da Gama then had him seized and beaten until he confessed his true mission. The man then admitted that the "whole country was ill-disposed" toward the Christians and that preparations were underway to attack them. Under more strident questioning, and some torture, the man also admitted that he had been sent to gauge the strength of da Gama's ships and weapons. He was released but confined aboard the *São Gabriel*. This man would later admit that he had hoped to entice the Portuguese to Goa, where the Muslim ruler planned to use them in his own wars with neighboring kingdoms. He would make the return trip to Portugal, where he was baptized, took the name Gaspar da Gama, and would become a favorite of D. Manuel.

On October 5, 1498, the Portuguese, after burning their captured Indian ship, finally left Anjedive and began to traverse the Arabian Sea. The voyage, however, was a difficult one, lasting more than three months, with the weather alternating between dead calms and adverse winds. Da Gama learned another valuable lesson on this stage of the voyage: the importance of sailing to exploit the winds of the alternating monsoons in the Indian Ocean. Had the Captain-major waited for the favorable winds of the northeast monsoon in late December, the voyage would have been far quicker and less painful. Instead, these three months took a heavy toll. The fresh fruits and vegetables quickly ran out, the water became foul, and food began to run low. Worse, scurvy reappeared among the crews. About thirty men had been lost in the first outbreak on the African coast; another thirty perished in the second outbreak. By December, there were only seven or eight men fit to sail each of the ships. As the author of the *Roteiro* declared: "I assure you that if this state of affairs had continued for another fortnight, there would have been no men at all to navigate the ships."

Even though the situation was critical, da Gama once again proved his mettle and maintained discipline. The Captain-major also held a council with his officers, where they decided that "if a favorable wind enabled us we would return to India whence we had come." Fortunately, the monsoon winds ended the suffering of the fleet and the coast of Africa was sighted on January 2, 1499. Or as the *Roteiro* related: "But it pleased God in his mercy to send us a wind which, in the course of six days carried us within sight of land." The joy among the crews was immense: "at this we rejoiced as much as if the land we saw had been Portugal for with the help of God we hoped to recover our health there, as we had done once before." The Portuguese found themselves off Mogadishu, but they did not seek assistance in the Muslim town. On January 5, a storm badly damaged the *São Rafael*. Two days later, da Gama was forced to repel pirates off Pate. Finally, on January 7, Malindi was sighted, the place "where we wished to go."

The five-day stay at Malindi constituted a badly needed respite for the fleet. Fortunately, the sultan retained his friendship for the Portuguese: a sheep, oranges, fowl, eggs, and other provisions were obtained. These citrus fruits evidently came too late to save those with scurvy: "but our sick did not much profit by this, for the climate affected them in such a way that many of them died here." Da Gama sent the sultan a present and asked for a "tusk of ivory to be given to the King [D. Manuel], his Lord, and asking that a pillar be placed on the land as a sign of friendship." The sultan quickly agreed to these requests and also sent a young Muslim boy to the fleet to accompany it to Lisbon "in order that the King of Portugal might know how much he desired his friendship." The fleet departed from Malindi on January 11, passed by Mombasa, and anchored at the São Raphael shoals on Sunday, January 13. Here, Vasco da Gama, as his command had been reduced to less than 100 men, made the difficult decision to consolidate the fleet. Everything of use and value aboard the *São Rafael*, including its oak figurehead, which da Gama came to treasure, was divided among the *São Gabriel* and *Berrio*, and the *São Rafael* was burned. The two remaining ships passed Zanzibar, and on February 1 anchored off the island of São Jorge near Mozambique. The following day, a *padrão* was set up, and a mass was said for the crews on the same spot as on the outward voyage. The Cape of Good Hope was doubled on March 20, 1499. "Those who had come so far were in good health and quite robust, although at times nearly dead from the cold winds which we experienced."

After passing the Cape of Good Hope, the ships had twenty-seven days of favorable winds and reached the Cape Verde Islands by April 16. Nearing the Guinea coast on April 25, the main source for the events of the voyage, the *Roteiro*, abruptly ends. Perhaps its author decided to remain at one of the Portuguese possessions on that coast, and the original manuscript that was later transcribed and copied ended at this point. In any case, the less reliable chronicler accounts and other documents that have survived from the summer of 1499 make it possible to complete the final events in the voyage. Shortly after April 25, the *São Gabriel* and *Berrio* were separated in a storm. Nicolau Coelho, perhaps in an effort to "steal the thunder" from da Gama, headed to Lisbon alone as quickly as possible. The *Berrio*, in fact, reached the Tagus in Lisbon on July 10, 1499, after a voyage of 732 days. Da Gama, after waiting a day for the *Berrio*, put in at the island of Santiago. There, he turned over command of the *São Gabriel* to João de Sá, with orders to make for Lisbon as quickly as possible.

Paulo da Gama was gravely ill, most probably in the final stages of tuberculosis, and his brother evidently wanted to arrange an even quicker passage for him to Portugal in the hope that his life might be saved or, failing that, he would not have to be buried at sea. Vasco da Gama chartered a swift caravel and began this voyage, only to find that his brother's condition worsened. The caravel put in at Angra on the island of Teixeira in the Azores. There, Paulo da Gama died "as the very good Christian that he was," and he was buried with all possible honors. The exact date that João de Sá and the *São Gabriel* reached Lisbon is not definitively recorded. It was probably in early August and definitely before the twenty-eighth of that month. Similarly, the exact date of the triumphal return of Vasco da Gama to Lisbon is also subject to debate; the generally accepted date is sometime between August 29 and September 14, 1499. The epic voyage that had discovered the sea route around Africa to the riches of the Indian Ocean trade, and in the process extended the fight against Islam, had been successfully completed. Nevertheless, an even more vital question remained; how would both Portugal and Vasco da Gama seek to exploit this historic achievement?

IV

The Spoils of Success: Wealth, Fame, and a Second Voyage to India, 1499–1503

"We hope, with the help of God, that the great trade which now enriches the Moors of those parts [India] . . . shall, in consequence of our regulations be diverted to the natives and ships of our own kingdom." Letter from D. Manuel I to Ferdinand and Isabella, July 1499

Summary

The chapter details Vasco da Gama's reception in Lisbon upon his return from India and the rewards he received from D. Manuel. Portuguese efforts to exploit the sea route to India are examined, including Cabral's 1500 fleet, which discovered Brazil. Da Gama's second voyage to India in 1502 is also detailed. Based on the superior firepower of this large fleet, da Gama was able to adopt harsh methods in his relations with the sultan of Kilwa and the Zamorin of Calicut. His attempts to develop a regular trade with the Malabar ports of Cannanur and Cochin is described, as is his naval battle off Calicut with a Mappila fleet in February 1503.

Da Gama's Reception in Lisbon, Significance of His First Voyage

Vasco da Gama, after overseeing the burial of his brother Paulo, reached Lisbon in mid-September 1499. When

71

D. Manuel I received word that his Captain-major was at Belém, he ordered several leading nobles to conduct da Gama to his presence. When this delegation reached the palace, "it was difficult to arrive because of the multitude of people gathered to see a sight so novel to them as Vasco da Gama appeared to them." Why? "Because he had done such a great thing as discovering India but also because everyone thought he was dead." Unlike the perplexing questions that had marred Columbus's return earlier that decade, there was no doubt that da Gama had indeed reached the ultimate goal of nearly a century of Portuguese expansion: India. Much has been made of the importance of the voyage of 1497–1499. Some historians have stressed the meeting of the Mediterranean, Atlantic, and Indian Ocean trading systems. Others have detailed how the voyage signaled a crucial outflanking of Islam in the continuing crusade against the Moors. Some scholars have viewed da Gama's achievement as the first step in an inexorable shift in European economic power from the Italian city-states to Iberia and eventually the northern Atlantic capitalist powers of England and the Netherlands. As the great eighteenth-century physiocrat Adam Smith asserted in *Wealth of Nations* (1776): "The discovery of America, and that of a passage to the East Indies by the Cape of Good Hope, are the two greatest and most important events recorded in the history of mankind." For Smith, da Gama's sea route to Asia "opened, perhaps, a still more extensive range to foreign commerce than even that of America."

On his first voyage, da Gama had proven both himself and the wisdom of his selection as Captain-major of the fleet during the hardships of the voyage. His iron will, stubbornness, and resolve had overcome many difficulties. The return voyage to India was one of the greatest feats of seamanship in recorded history, far surpassing that of Columbus in time, miles covered, nautical difficulty, and immediate commercial significance. His crusade for D. Manuel had indeed been a success. Da Gama had also made sure to return with material evidence of his success: the spices and precious stones aboard the *São Gabriel* and *Berrio* confirmed the wealth of India, while Monçaide and Gaspar da Gama could attest to his report and future potential benefits for the Crown.

Those at court less than enamoured with the India project, however, did point out that less than half the original crew had returned and that the quantity of Indian trading goods obtained was less than impressive. D. Manuel, and a great majority of the Portuguese people, who were all impressed that such a small group of dedicated men could have accomplished so much, dismissed these criticisms. From the outset, the deeds of da Gama and his men were the stuff of legend. Indeed, by the end of the century, the great Portuguese poet, Luís Vaz de Camões, would turn da Gama and his men into Homeric heroes in his epic poem the Os Lusíadas. Yet, in the late summer of 1499, several pivotal questions confronted D. Manuel. How much had really been achieved by da Gama's voyage? What was the best course of action to exploit his initial success? How should the king reward the Captain-major for his services?

No records have survived on the meeting between D. Manuel and da Gama in September 1499. Nevertheless, both men were probably elated at the outcome of the voyage. After all, for the king, the wealth of the spice trade signaled his rise into the ranks of the most powerful rulers in Europe, while for his Captain-major it promised his rise into the ranks of the most powerful nobles in Portugal. Even before da Gama had reached Belém, D. Manuel, relying on Nicolau Coelho's account, had written three letters announcing news of the success of the voyage to his parents-in-law, Ferdinand and Isabella, to Cardinal D. Jorge da Costa in Rome, and to Pope Alexander VI. "Your Highnesses already know that we had ordered Vasco da Gama, a nobleman of our household, and his brother Paulo da Gama, with four vessels to make discoveries by sea, and that two years have now elapsed since their departure." In the letters, D. Manuel noted that "as the principal motive of this enterprise has been, with our predecessors, the service of God our Lord, and our own advantage, it pleased him in His mercy to speed them on their route." Da Gama had discovered India "and other kingdoms and lordships bordering upon it."

There, he had found "large cities, large edificies, and rivers, and great populations, among whom is carried on all the trade in spices and precious stones," which were carried in ships to Mecca, "and thence to Cairo, whence they are dispersed throughout the world." Samples of cinnamon, cloves, ginger, nutmeg, and pepper had been obtained, "as had many fine stones of all sorts such as rubies." Da Gama, moreover, had evidently found many Christians in India. While these co-religionists were "not yet strong in the faith or possessed of a thorough knowledge of it," once properly "fortified in the faith, there will be an opportunity for destroying the Moors of those parts." D. Manuel believed "with the help of God, that the great trade which now enriches the Moors of those parts, through whose hands its passes without the intervention of other persons or peoples," could, with Portuguese intervention, "be diverted to the natives and ships of our own kingdom."

D. Manuel Rewards Himself and da Gama

The king's joy over the success of da Gama's voyage was reflected over the next few years in both symbolic and concrete acts. As early as his letter of August 28, 1499, to D. Jorge da Costa in Rome, D. Manuel signaled his newfound status among the kings of Europe. He began by claiming a new title for himself: "Dom Manuel, by the Grace of God King of Portugal and of the Algarves on this side of and beyond the sea, in Africa, Lord of Guinea and of the Conquest the Navigation and Commerce of Ethiopia, Arabia, Persia, and India." The king also ordered a new gold coin of 712 grams and a value of ten *cruzados* struck to commemorate the voyage. Convinced of the wealth that would soon be flowing in from the India trade, D. Manuel also began an impressive campaign of public works. New buildings were started along the Tagus River relating to the envisioned India trade, including the royal dockyards, the India House, and the royal warehouses. The most impressive of these new projects was the building of a new church of the Jeronimos at Belém near the chapel where da Gama had prayed the night before his departure. The lands near Restello were obtained and given to the "principal and brothers of Sao Jeronymo, the saint to whom the king paid his personal devotion, so that they might erect a monastery where in addition to their original statues they would offer prayers for the soul of the Infante Henry."

Construction on this monument to the discovery of India began in late 1499.

While D. Manuel was busy exploiting the success of the 1497–1499 voyage for the glory of his reign and kingdom, Vasco da Gama was similarly involved in the process of seeking to reap the benefits of his personal achievements. One of the more highly debated aspects of da Gama's life is his relationship with D. Manuel following the return from his first voyage. While D. Manuel did not have a reputation as a particularly generous king, it appears that he made a sincere effort to reward the Captain-major for his considerable services. This is not to say, however, that the king did not use the same Machiavellian criteria in making such rewards as he did with any noble. Da Gama, by virtue of his accomplishments, had eclipsed all the previous services offered by his family to the Crown in its slow rise in the nobility. Such accomplishments clearly merited rewards far above what previous men serving the Crown in the process of expansion could command. Moreover, da Gama, at the outset of the voyage, already came from a higher social status than men like Bartolomeu Dias, thanks to the work of his grandfather and father. In short, his background and the nature of his mission were demonstrably different from these earlier royal servants. For all of these reasons, the rewards would also have to be far more substantial. Another annual pension (*tença*) would not do. Throughout the fall of 1499, da Gama waited with high expectations. As is usually the case in such circumstances, da Gama could probably never have been granted all that he thought he deserved. This reality would eventually lead to friction with the king.

Controversy Over the Lordship of Sines

D. Manuel apparently asked da Gama what he desired. Predictably, the Captain-major asked for something closest to his heart: He petitioned the king for the seignory or lordship of Sines, his birthplace and the place where his father had been *alcaide-mor*. D. Manuel had no problem with this compensation. Logistically and politically, however, such a grant was fraught with difficulties. Sines and most of the surrounding region belonged to the Order of Santiago, of which the duke of Coimbra, D. Jorge, the bastard son of D. João II, still served as Grand Master. Either thinking that the traditional ties of the da Gama family could overcome this problem, or in an attempt to force da Gama into choosing between allegiance to the Order of Santiago or Christ, D. Manuel honored this request. On December 24, 1499, he declared: "To whoever sees this our Patent, bearing in mind the merits of Vasco da Gama, noble of our household, and of the many services that he has performed for us in the discovery of the Indies, we have decided to give, gift, and grant him the town of Sines, by sworn right and as heritable property, with its revenues and taxes, save God's tithe on the sea and on the land, and with civil and criminal jurisdiction over it." Seeking to address the main problem at hand, D. Manuel continued: "before we can give him the formal letter of transfer, we must first give satisfaction for it to the said Order, after receiving dispensation from the Holy Father, compensating it with another town belonging to the Crown." Compensation would also have to be given to the current holder of the commandery and *alcaide-mor* D. Luis de Noronha. Despite these obstacles, da Gama sought to have the terms of this grant fulfilled.

Alexander VI granted papal dispensation in 1501. Yet, suitable compensation for both the Order of Santiago and D. Luis de Noronha was difficult to arrange. The commandery of Sines belonged to the so-called "Master's table" of the Order, thus giving D. Jorge considerable power in determining its fate. The stakes in material terms were relatively high because Sines generated a good deal of revenue for the Order of Santiago and its commander. According to a list of commanders for the early sixteenth century, the largest annual pension for this period was perhaps 800,000 *reais*. Da Gama already enjoyed 80,000 *reais* from his grants of Mouguelas and Chouparria. Sines yielded Noronha some 150,000 *reais* with perhaps another 50,000 *reais* coming to him from the shipyard of the port. Complicating da Gama's task was the fact the Noronha came from an extremely powerful family at court and in the Order of Santiago, with more than sufficient weight to resist any demand for Sines.

D. Luis de Noronha was the natural son of D. Sancho de Noronha, count of Odemira, one of the leading members of Portuguese society during the reign of D. Afonso V, as well as a leading member of the Order of Santiago. His kinsman, D. Pedro de Noronha, served as *commendador-mor* of the Order. Vasco da Gama may have badly wanted the town, but Noronha was determined to hold it, and bad blood quickly developed in Sines. In one incident, a slave of D. Luis was slashed on the arm and shoulder with a sword wielded by Alvaro Afonso, a servant of da Gama. Clearly, the intrigues of court and military politics were conspiring to delay, if not deny, the one demonstration of Crown patronage that Vasco da Gama truly desired.

Other Rewards for Vasco da Gama

In the meantime, D. Manuel bestowed other forms of recognition and wealth on the discoverer of the sea route to India. On January 10, 1500, the king gave da Gama the much-coveted right to use the title of **Dom** and to attend the royal council. He also extended this socially significant title to Vasco's youngest brother, Aires; his sister, Teresa (Dona); and their descendants. D. Manuel also gave da Gama an annual pension of 300,000 *reais* in perpetuity derived from fishing tithes and excise revenues in Sines and surrounding towns. It is significant that financially this grant surpassed what da Gama would have received from the disputed lordship of Sines. Moreover, it gave him a further vested interest in the immediate area surrounding Sines, an area long dominated by the Order of Santiago.

This letter also gave D. Vasco the right to bring 200 *cruzados* in spices from India each year and to sell them in Portugal without paying custom duties, save that of the *vintena* (5%) for the Order of Christ. Yet, perhaps the most impressive piece of largesse in this document was the concession to da Gama of the title Admiral of the Sea of India with all the substantial "honors, prerogatives, liberties, power, jurisdiction, revenues, quitrents, and duties" that by longstanding decree were enjoyed by the Admiral of Portugal. This office dated back to at least 1288 and wielded great powers over the fleets of the kingdom. From this point, there were now two Admirals of Portugal: one for the Atlantic and the other held by da Gama in the Indian Ocean. This grant formalized the multi-oceanic nature of the developing Portuguese empire in the wake of da Gama's first voyage.

Besides being of great immediate interest to da Gama, this royal letter of January 1500 is significant for several reasons. First, it showed that D. Manuel was anxious to compete with the claims and grants that Ferdinand and Isabella had made regarding Columbus. The monarchs of Castile and Aragon had given Columbus the title of Dom and the identical title of Admiral during their negotiations with him. In 1500, D. Manuel thus staked his claim for parallel power and authority in Asia as the Spanish monarchs had claimed in the New World. In doing so, the Portuguese king supported one of the most common, although flawed, interpretations of the Portuguese age of discoveries, namely, that the quest for India had been a vital component of this quest dating uninterrupted from the days of Prince Henry. As the king wrote, "The Infante D. Henrique my uncle, began the discovery of the land of Guinea, in the era of 1433 with the intention and desire that by that coast of the said Guinea of discovering and finding India." The objective for this kingdom was "obtaining the many riches that there are in it," and "for making the faith of Our Father in more places known." On February 22, 1501, D. Manuel sought to placate da Gama by granting him an additional annual pension of 1,000 *cruzados* "during the time that he shall not . . . be able to have the enjoyment of the town of Sines."

Da Gama's Life in Portugal, 1499–1501

Not much is known of da Gama's daily life from 1499 through 1501. He probably lived in Évora, but spent time in both Lisbon and in the area near Sines, where his revenues were based. Evidently not all of the promised monies from the king were promptly paid. In November 1501, in lieu of a full cash payment for his 70,000 *reais*, D. Vasco was given a quantity of wheat in its place. D. Manuel's order to his treasurer for this wheat, valued at 28,000 *reais*, and bearing da Gama's receipt, still exists. This document contains one of only three signatures of D. Vasco to have survived the ravages of time. "I, Dom Vasco da Gama, declare that it is true that I have received the said 15 *moios* of wheat from the said Go. De Sequeira. Dom Vasco da Gama." A grant of 1501 also nominated D. Vasco as *capitão-mor* of the armadas sent to India. As D. Manuel wrote: "All of the armadas which we shall order made . . . during his lifetime for the said ports of India, whether they only be for traffic in merchandise or whether it is necessary to make war . . . he [da Gama] may take the chief captaincy of them and when he thus wishes . . . we may not place in them or appoint another chief captain except him." These monetary and honorific grants from the Crown established da Gama's fortune and reflected his fame. Nevertheless, he was also determined to solidify his own noble house and family after his return from India.

Da Gama accomplished this vital task by embracing the time-honored technique of arranging a socially advantageous marriage using his newfound fame and fortune as collateral. Sometime between 1500 and 1501, D. Vasco da Gama married **Dona Catarina de Ataíde**. Dona Catarina was the daughter of Álvaro de Ataíde and Dona Maria da Silva. Her late father had been *alcaide* of Alvor, and D. João II had died in his manor house in 1495. This marriage produced six sons and a daughter: Francisco da Gama, **D. Estêvão da Gama**, D. Pedro da Silva, Paulo da Gama, Christavão da Gama, Alvaro de Ataíde, and Isabel de Ataíde. This marriage also opened important family connections for da Gama. His new wife was a first cousin to the powerful Almeida family. This clan of cousins included the count of Abrantes, D. Jorge de Almeida, *commendador-mor* of the Order of Aviz, and **D. Francisco de Almeida**, who would serve as the first Viceroy of India. About this time, the Almeidas, the Ataídes, and the da Gamas all sought to distance themselves from D. Jorge and the Order of Santiago in favor of cultivating closer ties to the king and the Order of Christ. Before his departure for India in 1505, D. Francisco de Almeida shifted his allegiance to the Order of Christ.

D. Manuel Consolidates Portugal's Position in the Indian Ocean

While da Gama was busy solidifying his family life and fortune, D. Manuel exploited the opportunities presented by the success of the 1497–99 voyage. Some of his councilors still argued against creating an Asian empire given the kingdom's relatively meager resources and the comparative power of Islam in the Indian Ocean basin. The king, however, once again brushed aside such doubts. In D. Manuel's view, God himself had helped guide da Gama to India and back, and he wanted Portugal to rule over parts of Asia, converting its peoples to the Catholic faith. The king realized that da Gama's success had served as a call to action for the Muslim powers and Arab traders from Egypt to Indonesia, who then controlled the trade, as well as to the Italians, who had grown rich as middlemen on the traditional caravan routes in the eastern Mediterranean.

As early as the summer of 1499, the mood in northern Italy had grown decidedly anxious. "As soon as the news [of da Gama's return] reached Venice, the populace was thunderstruck, and the wiser among them regarded the news as the worst they could have received." It was therefore vital to send a large expedition to establish a Portuguese presence at key points along the east African coast and in India before any other European powers could enter the trade and before the Muslims and Italians could prepare an effective response. To lead this expedition, D. Manuel selected **Pedro Álvares (de Gouveia) Cabral.** Cabral had been born in 1467(?) into a minor noble family. He had been a page in the court of D. João II and later became a gentleman of the king's council and a member of the Order of Christ. Strangely, there is no evidence that Cabral either had any substantial nautical experience before 1500 or ever made another voyage after his return to Lisbon. This was purely a political appointment by the king. Since da Gama was actively involved in preparing instructions for Cabral, selecting the officers of the expedition as well as outfitting the fleet, he evidently approved of the selection. Cabral also had the respect of his officers and men, including some of the most seasoned mariners of the day, such as, Bartolomeu Dias and Duarte Pacheco Pereira.

Cabral's Voyage of 1500-1501 and the Discovery of Brazil

Cabral's powerful fleet included thirteen ships. These vessels were larger and better armed than those of 1497. The tonnage of these ships was more than five times that of the first India fleet. D. Manuel, with the assistance of da Gama, provided Cabral with precise sailing instructions, a large cargo for trade, rules and regulations for the fleet, as well as suitable presents for indigenous rulers in Africa and India. The king also provided a formal letter for the Zamorin of Calicut. This letter clearly shows that the Portuguese elite still wanted to believe that the Zamorin and his people were indeed Christians. It offered friendship and trade, but also contained a threat that Cabral's firepower could more than back up. "Our set purpose is to follow the will of God rather than of men, and not to fail through any opposition to prosecute this enterprise and continue our navigation, trade, and intercourse in these lands which the Lord God desires to be served newly by our hands, not wishing that our labors to serve Him be in vain." Cabral's squadron also carried three royal traders or factors; pilots; clerks; interpreters, including Monçaide and the five Hindus taken by da Gama; as well as an astronomer. The success of the 1497 voyage resulted in a surplus of volunteers in 1500, who this time received a fixed pay, for the expedition. D. Manuel, on the advice of D. Vasco, also sent sufficient and appropriate gifts and barter goods: two boatloads of trinkets for the African trade and copper, vermilion, mercury, amber, coral, woolens, satins, and velvets for India. Venetian coinage was also entrusted to Cabral. Overall, the second India fleet carried close to 1500 men.

By early March 1500, the fleet had assembled off Belém. One of Cabral's ships, the *Annunciada*, was owned by Bartholomo Marchioni, a Florentine who had helped arrange letters of credit for Covilhā and Paiva more than a decade earlier. After Cabral received his banner and formal instructions from D. Manuel, and a mass was held, the ships departed on March 9. On March 23, one ship was lost. By April 22, 1500, however, the coast of Brazil was sighted and claimed for D. Manuel. Cabral sent a ship back to Lisbon announcing this discovery and remained on the coast until early May. The passage across the Atlantic for the remaining eleven ships was slow and difficult. A comet sighted on May 12 was judged as an ill omen for the fleet, and this belief was seemingly justified when a fierce storm battered and scattered the fleet on May 24. Four ships were lost in this storm, including that of the great explorer and navigator Bartholomeu Dias, who went down with his ship. Cabral's flagship and two other ships doubled the Cape of Good Hope and were joined in Mozambique by three others. The remaining ship, under Diogo Dias, spent time on the island of Madagascar and in the Red Sea before rejoining Cabral on the return passage home.

Ten days were spent refitting in Mozambique. The sultan, still evidently humbled by da Gama's show of force, treated the Portuguese well. Cabral's fleet then sailed for Kilwa. There, the powerful sultan refused to sign a treaty with the Portuguese and treated them rudely. Cabral and the fleet anchored in the friendly confines of Malindi on August 1, 1500. After taking on supplies and capable pilots, the six ships traversed the Arabian Sea and anchored off Calicut on September 13. Cabral fired a salute and soon learned that the old Samudri, the eighty-fourth of his line, had died. A young, more dynamic Zamorin had recently taken power, and he was eager to develop his domains and trade at the expense of rival Hindu coastal kingdoms like Cochin.

Cabral's Violent Visit to the Malabar Coast

Cabral's stay in Calicut was anything but productive. Mutual suspicions and mistrust characterized the visit from the start. All of the Hindu hostages except one were ignored upon their return because they were from a lower caste than da Gama had been told. Cabral, in turn, demanded hostages while negotiations took place with the Zamorin, and five Brahmins were sent out. Initially, a house and warehouse were also provided for the Portuguese, but events soon turned ugly. Ayres Correira, the factor ashore, awoke on the night of December 16, 1500, to find the Portuguese ashore under attack from Arabs, Kerala Muslims, and Hindus. The compound was abandoned, but of the eighty men ashore, at least forty were killed within, and another fourteen on the retreat to the beach. Less than thirty Portuguese, most badly wounded, reached Cabral's ships. Ayres Correira was among the casualties, and his young son barely escaped with his life.

The exact reasons for this attack are not clear. According to some sources, Correira had advised Cabral to seize a Muslim-owned ship leaving for the port of Jiddah, which he saw as violating the pledge of the Zamorin to give the Portuguese preference in loading a cargo of spices. In retaliation, the Arabs of Calicut had launched the attack. This unfortunate massacre, for which the Samudri offered no explanation, ended any hope for peaceful relations with Calicut. In revenge, Cabral seized and burned at least ten Arab ships anchored before the town and then bombarded both Calicut and Pantalayani to great effect. He then sailed for Cochin.

The ruler of Cochin, Unni Goda Varma, badly wanted an ally against the Samudri. He was therefore much more gracious to Cabral, and a rich cargo of pepper, cinnamon, porcelain, and cotton textiles was soon obtained. Cabral also accepted two of the king's servants as ambassadors for the return voyage to Portugal. He also left some of his men behind to begin the process of setting up a factory in Cochin. In mid-January, Cabral stopped in Cannanur, where he was well received by the Kolattiri Raja and even more cinnamon was purchased. The fleet then began the return voyage to Lisbon.

Off Mozambique, the ship of the vice-commander of the fleet, Sancho de Tovar, ran aground. Shortly after leaving Mozambique, the fleet was again scattered in a storm. But between late June and late July 1501, Cabral's five remaining ships reached Lisbon. These ships carried some 4000 *cantari* of goods, mainly pepper. The sale of this cargo, even considering the ships lost, not only reimbursed D. Manuel and the others for their investment but returned close to 100% profit. The king and da Gama were overjoyed at this result. D. Manuel, believing the India trade was within his grasp, boasted that the Venetians should thereafter consider sending their vessels to Lisbon for spices. Yet, Cabral's voyage still left many questions unanswered for the Portuguese with respect to the Asian spice trade. After all, relations with the Zamorin were terrible, the factory at Cochin was only tenuously established, while the Arabs and Muslims were still in control of the trade. How could this monopoly be broken? One of the Venetian Sernigi's 1499 letters on the formation of Cabral's fleet offered an early clue to the deliberations of D. Manuel and D. Vasco on this vital question. "If the king does not permit the Portuguese to trade in those countries, the captain of these ships carries orders to seize as many native ships as he can." By the late summer of 1501, it appears that both the Portuguese king and D. Vasco da Gama had decided to embrace open warfare to break Muslim dominance over the Indian Ocean trade. Therefore, preparations began for a large and powerful expedition that would break the stranglehold of the Arabs and Mameluke rulers of Egypt over this trade and divert it from the eastern Mediterranean routes to Lisbon via the Cape of Good Hope.

The Voyage of João de Nova, 1501–1502

In the meantime, another small expedition under **João de Nova** had departed in March 1501, bound for the Indian Ocean and charged with discovery and commerce. De Nova hailed from Galicia and had spent time in North Africa. At the time of his appointment to command the 1501 fleet, he held a relatively minor government position in Lisbon. He was probably chosen for this post thanks to his close friendship with the powerful noble **Tristão da Cunha**. Da Nova's fleet explored the Brazilian coast before touching at Kilwa, Mozambique, Mombasa, and Malindi on the east coast of Africa in June and July 1501. By November, the fleet reached Cannanur. There, de Nova received a friendly reception from the Kolattiri Raja, who offered him cargo. De Nova then headed for Cochin.

Although there are conflicting versions of de Nova's actions off the Malabar coast, he captured at least two and perhaps as many as four ships laden with cargo at Calicut, with one of these ships belonging to the Zamorin. At Cochin, the Portuguese factory was in tenuous shape due largely to a lack of interest in Iberian goods. De Nova had caused sufficient damage to the Zamorin's interests to prompt him to form a retaliatory fleet from Pantalayini. Once again, however, the superiority of Portuguese shipborne artillery was proven in an engagement fought in the waters north of Cochin in January 1502. De Nova then returned to Cannanur, where he took on a respectable cargo and deposited a handful of men to establish a permanent factory. Seeking to profit from the winds of the northeast monsoon, de Nova began his return voyage in February 1502. The fleet reached Lisbon in September of that year, carrying a cargo of around 1000 *cantari* of pepper, 500 *cantari* of cinnamon, and 50 *cantari* of ginger.

Da Gama's Second Voyage to India, 1502–1503

As da Nova's fleet departed from Cannanur, the large expedition that D. Manuel and D. Vasco had decided to send to entrench Portuguese power in the Asian trade departed from Lisbon. The sixteenth-century Portuguese chroniclers all state that Pedro Álvares Cabral was originally chosen to command this fourth Indian fleet of 1502. Yet, by the time of its sailing, D. Vasco da Gama, Admiral of the Indian Sea, had assumed command. There were several factors involved in this change of command. First, as the king discussed the formation of the fleet in late 1501, he concluded that this expedition, especially in light of Cabral's experience in Calicut, should have an overwhelmingly military function. Revenge against the Zamorin had to be exacted, the bothersome Arab and Muslim traders entrenched along the Malabar coast would have to be taught a harsh lesson, and regular sailing between the Red Sea and India would have to be halted. As Alberto Cantino, an agent for the duke of Ferrara in Lisbon, wrote at this time, the object of this fleet was "to guard and defend the mouth of the Red Sea, so that the ships of the Sultan could not pass between Mecca to Calicut carrying spices." For this type of work, D. Vasco's previous deeds made him the obvious choice.

Second, D. Vasco enjoyed great prestige and power with D. Manuel at this time. He also possessed the king's grant of 1501 as *Capitão-mor* of the armadas of India. This grant allowed him to assume command of any voyage sent to Asia during his lifetime. Relieving Cabral of his command was therefore entirely within his rights. Third, the king also decided on a divided fleet and command structure. Cabral may not have accepted this arrangement, especially when he learned that **Vincent Sodré**, D. Vasco's uncle, would command one of these squadrons and Estêvão da Gama, his cousin, the other. This arrangement had obvious appeal for da Gama. Finally, we should not make too much of this shift in command. Such last-minute changes were common during this period. In fact, a Cabral–da Gama–Cabral shift had probably occurred with respect to the command of the 1500 fleet.

In its final form, the 1502 expedition was divided into three squadrons. The largest, under D. Vasco's immediate command, consisted of ten ships. Vincent Sodré's squadron was made up of five ships; and his orders called for this squadron to cruise the Arabian Sea and Indian Ocean, intercepting as much Arab shipping as possible, thus crippling Muslim seaborne trade. The squadron under Estêvão da Gama, also consisting of five ships, had orders to remain in India and protect growing Portuguese interests there.

D. Vasco's rise in the hierarchy at court with respect to Asian affairs, as well as his ability to promote his own interests and those of his extended family, were admirably reflected in the 1502 fleet. He had overall command of this divided fleet, while all of his subordinate commanders were members of his own family, and many of these men had ties to the Order of Santiago. By including them, perhaps D. Vasco hoped for better treatment from Palmela toward his claim to Sines after his return. Together, da Gama and his kinsmen were determined to ensure that the interests of the Crown, and, by extension, of their own family, were promoted. This was a neat, albeit nepotistic, arrangement of the type characteristic of the period. As is the case for the 1497 voyage, no record of the 1502 voyage written by da Gama has been found. The only handwritten document by D. Vasco for the 1502 fleet is a six-page letter containing his instructions for Portuguese vessels arriving at the African city-state of Kilwa.

There are four main contemporary sources for da Gama's second voyage. The first is a short description compiled by a Flemish sailor aboard the fleet that was first published in 1504 with the title *Calcoen* (Calicut). The second is an account written by Tomé Lopes, who served as a clerk aboard a ship in Estêvão da Gama's squadron. There is also the account written by Mateo di Begnino, a factor for the Venetian Francesco Affaitato in Lisbon, who also served on one of Estêvão da Gama's ships. Begnino spent two months in the spring of 1503 in Mozambique compiling his account of the voyage. Finally, there is a brief anonymous manuscript account in Portuguese.

From Lisbon to the Cape of Good Hope, April to June 1502

On January 30, 1502, D. Vasco da Gama received his formal commission and royal standard from D. Manuel. Alberto Cantino's detailed description of this ceremony has survived. "The aforesaid Vasco wearing a long surtout of crimson satin of the French type, lined with ermine, and a beret and tunic matching the surtout, and adorned with a neck chain of gold, placed himself at the side of the king, who was surrounded by his entire court." After the virtues of both the king and his new Admiral had been declared to all those present, the herald-at-arms held out a book in his hand. D. Vasco swore eternal fidelity to the king and his descendants. He then knelt before the prince, who drew a ring from his own hand and slipped it on his finger. Da Gama had come far in the five years since his first voyage. His rich clothing reflected the wealth he had rapidly accumulated. His investiture by the king as Admiral of Portugal and Captain-major of the fleet of 1502 showed that he held a preeminent position at court with respect to Asian affairs. By February 10, the first two squadrons of the fleet had sailed. Estêvão da Gama's ships departed only on April 1, 1502. D. Manuel had made a notable investment in manpower and firepower in this fleet and expected a sizable return for his troubles. The initial successes of the Indian Ocean enterprise had to be consolidated and Muslim power in the trade destroyed. As commander, the pressure of all these expectations fell upon Vasco da Gama, who would once again prove himself more than adequate for a great challenge.

The two squadrons stopped briefly at the Canary Islands before heading southeast to Cape Verde, where wood and water were taken on. While there, a Portuguese vessel arrived "bringing 250 marks of gold, all in bracelets and jewels, which the blacks were accustomed to wear." This unexpected arrival furnished da Gama with a powerful weapon in the propaganda war that the Portuguese were waging with Venice at the time. Da Gama's squadron carried three ambassadors from India who had traveled to Lisbon with Cabral: one from the Kolattiri Raja of Cannanur and two from the king of Cochin. During their stay in Portugal, Venetian agents there had tried their best to undermine the impression of the kingdom as a rich and powerful one, which deserved a meaningful share of the India trade. D. Vasco ordered the ship's treasure displayed for these ambassadors. He then informed them that "ordinarily 12 to 15 ships brought a like quantity of gold each year to Dom Manuel, King of Portugal and Lord of Mina." This display impressed the Indians, who admitted that the Venetians had represented the conditions "far otherwise to them, but now they had seen for themselves and believed the words of da Gama."

The Swahili Coast of Africa

After rounding the Cape of Good Hope, da Gama's squadron spent most of June 1502 cruising off the southeast coast of Africa. Sofala's (*Safla* in Arabic=low ground) low-lying and unhealthy climate was partially offset by its potentially rich trade in gold from the interior kingdom of the Monomotapa. D. Vasco did his best to establish the Portuguese in this trade at Sofala. In twelve days (ca. June 14–26) the Portuguese obtained some 2,500 *misqâls* of this precious metal. Two of the Admiral's envoys were well received by the local ruler and soundings were taken of the port.

On June 26, D. Vasco's squadron headed for Mozambique island. While departing, D. Vasco's ship rammed another ship and, although the crew and cargo were offloaded, the ship had to be burned. At Mozambique, two ships that had been separated near the Cape of Good Hope rejoined the squadron. A caravel for trade along that coast was also constructed with wood brought from Portugal. A factor, with ten men to assist him, was installed for trading in the region, and Vicente Sodré's squadron joined the main fleet.

The combined fleet of D. Vasco and his uncle, made up of more than a dozen heavily armed ships, then made an impressive entrance into the harbor of the island of Kilwa, the most powerful Muslim city-state on that part of the African coast. Da Gama began his stay with a loud round of fire from his artillery, signaling his willingness to use military force to achieve his objectives. At Kilwa, the Admiral was determined to demonstrate both the power of his fleet and his king to the Muslims. Freed from the constraints of the limited resources of 1497, D. Vasco's true personality was at last revealed. The Admiral swiftly and decisively delineated his forceful strategy for entrenching Portugal in the trade and destroying Muslim power in that region. This was, after all, the main objective of his second voyage.

The Mahdali sultan of Kilwa in 1502 was Fuzail bin Sulaiman, but real power rested with Amir Ibrahim. Kilwa Kisiwani, the capital, was a rich and populous city. Its Great Mosque and palace overlooking the harbor were testaments to the wealth the sultanate had gained through its role as the entrepôt for the rich gold trade from inland Monomotapa to Sofala on the coast. Through Kilwa, in turn, luxury goods from China, India, and Arabia had traditionally reached the African interior, and huge profits were made. Fittingly, Kilwa had minted the first copper coinage in East Africa in the early thirteenth century. Probably unaware of this impressive history, but well versed in the details of Cabral's ill-treatment there, D. Vasco's opening gambit was simple and to the point: Submit to the Portuguese and pay a yearly tribute to D. Manuel or he would burn Kilwa Kisiwani to the ground. A letter from João da Nova fortified da Gama's resolve. This letter warned him of dealing with Amir Ibrahim and gave da Gama news of Portuguese interests at Calicut and Cannanur.

After the Portuguese cruised close to shore with their smaller vessels, Amir Ibrahim came out to parlay and D. Vasco obtained the formal homage he craved. As the Admiral wrote in one of his few extant letters: "I, Admiral Dom Vasco, and so forth, give notice to all captains whatever of ships of my Lord the King . . . that I came here the twelfth of the present month of July 1502, and wished to treat with the king, in order to establish peace and amity with him." Amir Ibrahim, however, "did not wish to treat with me, but treated me very discourteously." In such circumstances, and given the nature of his charge from D. Manuel, da Gama had few options. As he proudly declared: "I armed myself, together with all my people, prepared to destroy him, and drew up my vessels before his house and ran them up to the beach, and called upon him with far more rudeness than that with which he had met me." Amir Ibrahim had then seen that "it was in his interest to submit, and he came and I established peace and amity with him on the condition that he pay the King my Lord 1500 gold *misqâls* each year as tribute, and would pay at once the 1500 *misqâls* for the present year in which we are, and that he avow himself a vassal of His Highness."

Having achieved his major purpose in Kilwa, D. Vasco prepared to depart. He concluded his letter of July 20, 1502, with rendezvous instructions for Estêvão da Gama's ships. "I order you not to delay here, but at once go on to Melinde, and if you do not find me there, go on to Anjadiva, and if you do not find me there, go on to Cananor, and travel by day and night, taking rest so that you do not pass me, and if you do not find me there, in the same way go on to Calecut, and if you do not find me there either, go on to Cochim." This passage not only demonstrates the practical logistics of such expeditions in the early sixteenth century; it also shows that da Gama had a clear itinerary for the voyage from the outset.

On July 23, Estêvão da Gama and three ships reached Kilwa. The other two vessels had been separated in a storm. The combined fleet then sailed toward Malindi, but contrary winds convinced D. Vasco to begin the traverse of the Arabian Sea. This time he sailed on a more northerly route than in 1498. According to the Flemish author of the *Calcoen*, the Portuguese fleet made landfall in late August near Cambay, "a city of great commerce," located some 600 miles to the east of the "city of Mecca where is buried Mahomet the devil of the pagans." Sailing south, the fleet passed "a city called Oan [Goa or Honawar]" whose "king has at least 8000 cavalry and 700 war elephants," and anchored at Anjediva. There, "we took on water and wood, and we also took ashore our sick, at least three hundred of them, and there we killed a lizard [crocodile] which measured not less than five feet long." At Anjediva, the ship of Ruy Mendes de Brito joined the fleet with Tomé Lopes aboard. By early September, the last of Estêvão da Gama's ships had made their rendezvous with the fleet off Mount Eli. D. Vasco, thus reinforced, was both prepared and anxious to carry out the main points in his instructions.

Da Gama and the Burning of the Mîrî, September 1502

In early September, the Portuguese fleet neared the city of Cannanur. In a concise passage at this point in his narrative, the author of the *Calcoen* summarized the strategy that D. Vasco and his king had developed for breaking the power of the Muslims in the trade. "There [near Mount Eli] we awaited the ships from Mecca, since these are the ships which bring spices to our lands, and we wished to destroy them and thus the king of Portugal would make himself the sole master of the spices of the East." For the next few weeks, D. Vasco's fleet harassed Muslim shipping on the Malabar coast, capturing at least one richly loaded ship in the process. According to Tomé Lopes, on September 29, 1502, "several of our ships were cruising seeking those coming from Mecca, the *São Gabriel* encountered one from Calicut that was returning with two hundred and forty men, without counting women and children who were many, and all were returning from the said pilgrimage [to Mecca]." Lopes maintains that this ship carried "ten or twelve of the richest merchants of Calicut, among them one called Joar Afanquei [Jauhar al-Faqih?] and it is said that he was the factor of the Sultan of Mecca in the said city." Other accounts refer to this ship as the *Meri* or *Mîrî* and claim that it was owned by the Mamluk Sultan Qansawh al-Ghawri. All of the extant contemporary accounts, as well as later chroniclers, however, agree that D. Vasco captured and burned this ship. What is less certain is exactly how long and how difficult that process was for the Portuguese.

The anonymous Portuguese account was brief. "The ship *São Gabriel* sighted a ship, sailed over and captured it, and the ship was from Mecca, and it carried two hundred souls . . . they burnt and killed them all except 17 young boys who became Christians." Damião de Góis relates that the capture was only accomplished with "much work because the Muslims defended themselves very well all the said day and the following night." More than 300 of the enemy were killed and "several young boys in it Dom Vasco da Gama ordered taken to his ship, with the intention of making them friars at the Monastery of Our Lady of Belém."

By far the longest account of the capture was provided by Lopes. His account provided details of several futile attempts by D. Vasco to obtain the wealth of those aboard the ship; his attempts to set fire to the ship; and the brave resistance of the Muslims aboard, who were able to delay their ultimate fate for nearly a week. These encounters included a fierce hand-to-hand battle in which Lopes himself fought, while marveling at the bravery of his enemies, who battled as if "they did not feel their wounds." In the end, a Muslim traitor told the Admiral how to blow up the ship. "And thus, after all those combats, the Admiral had the said ship burnt with the men who were on it, very cruelly and without any pity." The author of the *Calcoen* reports this final act in much more laconic terms: "We took a ship from Mecca in which there were three hundred and eighty men and many women and children. And we took from it some twelve thousand *ducats* and another ten thousand in goods and we burnt the ship and all those people with gunpowder on the first day of October."

Da Gama's harshness on this occasion did not upset or surprise his sixteenth-century contemporaries, who understood the nature of warfare in that age, particularly when it involved the forces of Christianity and Islam. Turkish atrocities to Christians in the aftermath of the fall of Constantinople in May 1453 had been well publicized throughout Europe during da Gama's youth. Barros claims that D. Vasco felt particular antipathy once one of his retainers was crushed between the *Mîrî*'s hull and that of his own flagship early in the operation. In a letter that he wrote to the Samudri soon after, the Admiral explained his actions. "The men [on the *Mîrî*] were killed on account of the forty or so Portuguese who had been killed in Calecut, and the children baptized on account of a [Portuguese] boy, who the Moors had taken to Mecca to make a Moor . . . this was a demonstration of the manner that the Portuguese had in amending the damage that they had received, and the rest would be in the city if Calecut itself." Some historians have decried this "ineffaceable stain on the grim character of Dom Vasco da Gama." In fact, D. Vasco had operated not only in a predictable fashion given his character, but one that accorded with his instructions from D. Manuel. The purpose of his second fleet was in part to avenge the slights afforded Cabral in Kilwa and the massacre in Calicut. In carrying out this mission, the Admiral was expected to punish the rulers responsible but by extension also begin the process of destroying Muslim commercial power along the Indian coast and on the Indian Ocean. In attempting to instill fear and respect among his many enemies in Africa and Asia, such harsh methods were to be expected.

Searching for Allies at Cannanur, October 1502

Following the itinerary he had outlined in his letter at Kilwa, D. Vasco's fleet next stopped at Cannanur on October 18. The Kolattiri, in a quest for allies against the Samudri of Calicut, was amenable to the Portuguese from their arrival on that coast. The Portuguese fleet spent four days anchored before the town. According to the author of the *Calcoen*, "we bought all kinds of spices, and the king received us in great state and brought . . . two elephants and other strange animals which I cannot name." D. Vasco, anxious to demonstrate his newfound status and power, stood on a good deal of ceremony at Cannanur. After a rather exasperating series of negotiations, the Kolattiri was forced "to construct over the sea a very large wooden pier" for their formal meeting.

For this diplomatic encounter, da Gama had the poop of one of his ships "covered in velvet, half in crimson, and half in green, and placed on it the most important men of the fleet" all decked out in their finest clothing. The Admiral himself wore his finery as well in an effort to impress the rajah; his costly outfit was made of silk, with two large gold sashes. The Kolattiri, not to be outdone, arrived at the pier on a palanquin with four hundred retainers armed with swords. Gifts were then exchanged. The Admiral presented the local ruler with some branches of coral and silver and in return received precious stones. Da Gama sought to arrange a fair price for spices, but the Kollatiri informed him that he would send his merchants to arrange such matters the following day. When these men appeared, they were Muslim, and they quoted far higher prices than had previously been charged to the Portuguese. D. Vasco's anger over the Muslim duplicity frequently encountered on that coast quickly revealed itself. He sent a message to the Kolattiri questioning his true motives and threatening to return the spices with a few rounds from his ships that had already been loaded. Da Gama grudgingly allowed a factor to remain. But he instructed him to inform the local ruler that he would seek his cargo elsewhere and to warn him that if any Christian Portuguese on land were harmed or dishonored, "his Kafirs would pay for it." After delivering this warning, the Portuguese fleet sailed south on the October 22, 1502, toward Calicut.

While still anchored at Cannanur, the Admiral received two letters that provided him with valuable information on what awaited in Calicut. One of these letters was from Gonçalo Gil Barbosa at Cochin. The Samudri, like most of the rulers along the coast, had been warned of the powerful fleet D. Vasco possessed. For strategic reasons alone, he therefore sought peace with the Portuguese. A letter from the Samudri reached da Gama at this time, offering precisely this deal. The Hindu hierarchy in Calicut recognized that reprisals were likely both for having scorned the Admiral in 1498 and for allowing the massacre of Cabral's men to have taken place within the confines of the city in December 1500. Da Gama, as he anchored before Calicut in late October, possessed the avenging force he badly wanted in this longstanding feud with the Samudri.

Da Gama's maritime superiority allowed him to act from a position of strength throughout his second voyage. He had already captured and rather diplomatically released a large trading ship belonging to "Iuneos" (Jains or possibly Vanias) "people who traded marvelously in India, and control a great part of the spices." In contrast, an indigenous ship had been taken off Pantalayini. Two Muslims aboard the ship had been convicted of attacking Aires Correira's factory, based on testimony from the children taken from the *Mîrî*. These men had been hanged. During late October negotiations took place with Calicut. Envoys from the Samudri repeated his offer of peace to the Portuguese. They pointed out that the losses from Correia's factory had been compensated by goods from the ship Cabral had taken. The loss of Portuguese life had also been more than offset by Muslim losses on the *Mîrî* and da Gama's recent hangings. But D. Vasco, relishing his power, treated all these envoys with contempt. He told them that as a vassal of D. Manuel, he was a better man than the "betel-chewing" local ruler and that "his king could carve out a ruler equal to the Zamorin from the trunk of a palm tree." As his price for peace, the Admiral had merely one demand: Expel all Muslims from Calicut "for since the beginning of the world, the Moors have been the enemies of the Christians, and the Christians of the Moors."

The Samudri sought to drag out the negotiations, in part to complete a stockade of palm trees that he was constructing along the beach, reinforced by several artillery pieces. Da Gama, to show that he was deadly serious about his demand, began to capture local fishermen and others from passing boats. According to Lopes, some thirty-four of these men were hanged from the masts of the Portuguese ships. On November 1, the *São Jerónimo* and a caravel then fired on the crowd watching from the beach, and a general bombardment commenced, which lasted until nightfall and caused "very great destruction." According to Barros, "when night fell to speed things up and for greater terror, he [D. Vasco] had the heads, hands, and feet of the hanged men cut off, and put on a boat with a letter." Barros wrote that da Gama admitted that while these were not the men who had killed Cabral's crew, as relatives of the residents of the town, they had received this punishment. "The authors of that treachery could await a manner of death that was even more cruel."

According to Lopes's version, da Gama told the Samudri that if he expected peace he would have to pay for the goods "plundered in this port under your protection" as well as for the powder and shot he had used in the bombardment. The bodies of these men, or what was left of them, were thrown overboard so they would wash up on the beach for relatives to find. On November 3, the bombardment commenced again, with significant damage inflicted on the houses of the nobles located further from beach, "since those closer to the sea had already been destroyed." According to Lopes, as many as 400 cannonballs had been fired from the fleet by noon. D. Vasco and his ships easily repulsed a small fleet from shore that sought to halt this onslaught on the town.

Negotiations in Cochin, November 1502–January 1503

Later that day, D. Vasco left his uncle Vicente Sodré with seven ships to blockade Calicut and sailed with the rest of the fleet for Cochin. After reaching that port on November 7, the Admiral remained there for two months. Da Gama, recognizing the pivotal importance of Cochin for this phase of Portuguese commercial expansion, spent this time cultivating good relations with Unni Goda Varma. In mid-November, the Admiral went ashore and met with the local ruler. Da Gama presented the rajah with gifts of silver while Unni Goda Varma "gave the Admiral much jewelry, large and of great value, and also to the gentlemen and captains that had gone with him." Da Gama also gained favor by handing over three Muslims who twice tried to sell cows to the Portuguese for meat. As punishment and no doubt a warning, these men were impaled.

Thanks to his good working relationship with the Portuguese factors already operating in Cochin, da Gama was able to load an impressive cargo of spices. During this sojourn, the effectiveness of D. Vasco's ruthless policies on the Malabar coast was demonstrated. Three envoys from the Kolattiri of Cannanur arrived, informing the Admiral that spices sufficient to load two ships were available at market prices in Cochin. Da Gama promptly sent two ships north. After arriving from Calicut, Vicente Sodré was also sent north to load spices with three ships. On November 19, representatives of the so-called St. Thomas Christians of Mangalor and other places along the coast arrived. The Christian community along the entire western coast of India totaled perhaps 30,000 people. "They said that they were very satisfied, and content with our arrival in those parts of India, and that the Lord of the said country [Cranganor?] pledged obedience to the king of Portugal." These envoys questioned D. Vasco on matters of faith and told him of the great pilgrimages that these Christians made "to the tomb of the Apostle St. Thomas, that is found close to their land." Da Gama had at last found the Christians he sought. Based on the recommendations of these envoys, D. Vasco also sent three ships south to load spices in Kerala. As the author of the *Calcoen* described: "On the third January [1503] we departed for a city called Coloen [Kollam], where many good Christians came to meet us, who loaded our ships with spices. There are about 25,000 Christians who pay tribute like the Jews. There are about 300 Christian churches that have the names of the Apostles and other saints."

The Zamorin of Calicut also sent envoys to treat with da Gama during his stay in Cochin. On January 3, 1503, a Brahmin, with his son and two other men, arrived with a letter. Reflecting an awareness of Hinduism that was absent in 1498, Tomé Lopes declared: "these Brahmins are among us like the bishops, and priests, rich men who do not hold another office or charge except being honored by the people and given alms." They could travel anywhere with the utmost security since "no one would dare touch them even their enemies, or anyone in their company, because he would be deemed as damned and excommunicated." This Brahmin presented the Zamorin's letter, which offered peace and trade in Calicut should the Portuguese return. The ambassador, perhaps in an effort to convince da Gama of his trustworthiness, "brought with him very costly jewels worth 3000 *cruzados* in India, and he said to the Admiral that he wished to come with him to Portugal, and bring the said jewelry, and he asked permission to load some spices aboard our ships." D. Vasco in fact permitted the Brahmin to load 20 *bahars* of cinnamon aboard his flagship. On January 5, the Admiral embarked aboard Estêvão da Gama's ship, the *Flor de la Mar*, and sailed for Calicut. Upon doing so, he sent a caravel north to Cannanur with orders for his uncle Vicente Sodré to meet him off Calicut.

Diplomacy and Warfare on the Malabar Coast, 1503

This invitation of an alliance from the Zamorin, however, was a rather thinly disguised trap for da Gama. Soon after anchoring, the wealthy Brahmin went ashore and did not return. Another envoy appeared, however, and informed D. Vasco that the compensation in cash and spices that he had demanded for Cabral's losses was ready. All he needed to do was send a gentleman ashore to collect it. The Admiral, however, was not easily duped, and he flatly refused to comply. As a result, during the night, some seventy or eighty small boats loaded with soldiers surrounded and attacked the *Flor de la Mar*, attaching a second anchor on the ship to prevent it from escaping. Da Gama's cannons were useless to him in this fight, and a fierce hand-to-hand battle continued for several hours.

Vicente Sodré arrived early the next day with three ships. Nepotism indeed had its advantages. These reinforcements decided the issue: "the *paraus* [Indian warships] were dispersed and many men were killed." Da Gama wanted revenge for this ambush. He soon hung the Brahmin's son and two Nairs from the yardarms of his ship, paraded his victims before the town, and finally sent their corpses to the Zamorin with a letter in Malayalam. D. Vasco warned: "The punishment will be as you merit, and when I come back here, you will pay your dues, and not in money."

After a short stop in Cannanur, da Gama and Sodré returned to Cochin to complete the final stages of loading spices and to gather the entire fleet for the voyage home. Word soon reached D. Vasco that the Zamorin was assembling a fleet to attack the Portuguese. Aware that the favorable winds of the northeast monsoon demanded a prompt departure, da Gama nevertheless held additional negotiations with Unni Goda Varma in early

February. At these meetings, the local king agreed to a Portuguese factory with a factor with considerable powers over not only the Portuguese left behind but Indian Christians in the town as well. Formal letters were also compiled on behalf of Unni Goda Varma for D. Manuel confirming his desire for an alliance. Several envoys of Unni Goda Varma also embarked on the fleet. "On the tenth February 1503, on a Tuesday in the morning, we departed from the port of Cochim."

D. Vasco sailed north with ten fully laden ships and headed toward Cannanur to rendezvous with the three other Portuguese ships still taking on spices in that port. Off Calicut, the Portuguese fleet encountered the Mappila fleet assembled by the Zamorin, made up of at least thirty-two large ships carrying several hundred men in each, supported by a multitude of smaller craft. The Zamorin had done his best to outfit a fleet capable of defeating da Gama. The Arab traders in town had contributed little to this enterprise, and the Zamorin had thus been forced to pressure the Mappila community to bear this burden. In the end, a force containing nearly 7000 men had been assembled. As such, it probably embodied the most formidable Indian maritime force that the Malabar coast could muster against the Europeans in the early sixteenth century.

Even this formidable force, however, was no match for the superiority of the shipborne artillery of the Portuguese. The Mappila strategy was to close *en masse* upon da Gama's ships, hoping to negate his firepower. If they could grapple and board the Portuguese vessels, their overwhelming advantage in numbers would carry the day in hand-to-hand combat. This tactic, however, failed miserably. Da Gama was able to rain a fierce bombardment of cannonballs on the Zamorin's fleet. This move prevented his enemies from closing on his ships and inflicted heavy casualties in the process. Unable to withstand this bloody onslaught, the Mappila ships eventually turned and made for Calicut with the Portuguese in pursuit. As Da Gama's ships closed in, many of the enemies's crews simply jumped overboard into the rolling surf, hoping to escape. A heavy storm that night "brought a great fury of wind to the sea, which threw all the dead on land, and they had time to count them." Two enemy ships were captured and burned near the mouth of the

Calicut River "with us killing in those two boats more than three hundred." The Zamorin witnessed this debacle from one of his palaces. D. Vasco had won a great victory, a victory that foreshadowed even greater Portuguese naval victories in the Indian Ocean in the years to come. The Admiral and his fleet then sailed for Cannanur.

News of da Gama's great success had already reached Cannanur. Perhaps recognizing the new balance of power developing along the western Indian coast, many Mappila merchants had already decided to abandon Calicut in favor of towns allied to the Portuguese. As Tomé Lopes relates, the Portuguese received detailed intelligence on the Zamorin's fleet from these merchants. "This and many other things we learned from native merchants of Calicut who had fled, and came to live in Cananor because of the war we had brought, and they had taken with them their wives, and children, and all of their goods, because in Calicut they would have died of hunger." Bolstered by the fame of his victory, D. Vasco reconfirmed his alliance with the rajah, and he even extended it to a tripartite league with Cochin against Calicut. He also established a permanent factory in Cannanur of some twenty men. Finally reunited with his three ships that were taking on spices there, the Admiral was ready to depart by February 20, 1503. On that day, thirteen Portuguese ships, most heavily laden with spices, began the long voyage home. As D. Manuel had instructed, da Gama's maternal uncle, Vicente Sodré, and his brother Bras were left behind with five ships, the first permanent European naval presence in the Indian Ocean, to continue the policy of harassing Muslim shipping.

The Return Voyage to Portugal, April–October 1503

On the return voyage, D. Vasco decided to sail on a more direct route to Mozambique, which was reached on April 12. The remainder of the voyage home was exceedingly hard for the crews due to frequent storms and a lack of supplies. Da Gama dispatched the ships "two by two and three by three" once they

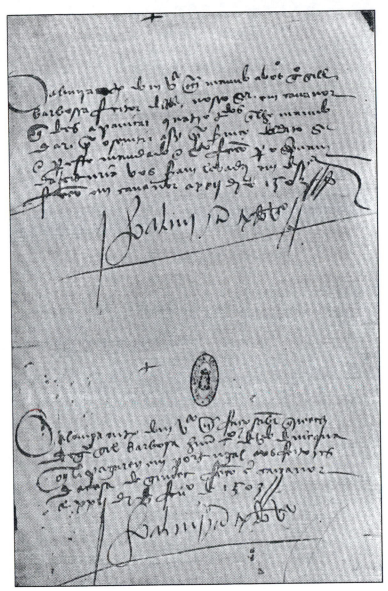

Order of D. Vasco da Gama to Goncalo Gil Barbosa, February 1503,
Arquivo Nacional da Torre do Tombo, CC II, Maço 7, Document 20.
(Glenn J. Ames)

had been careened and reprovisioned in Mozambique. The *São Gabriel* and *Santo Antonio* departed first on April 19 and were back in Lisbon by late August with news of da Gama's great triumphs: "in every place that he had been, either through love or through force, he had managed to do everything that he wanted." Appropriately, the Admiral departed with the last of his ships from southeast Africa in late June, reaching the Azores in late September. This Atlantic passage was especially harsh. According to an often-quoted section of the anonymous Portuguese account, this part of the voyage was accomplished only with the greatest difficulty "because so many of the crew were sick, that there were not enough to sail the ship, and neither the sick nor the rest had more to eat than biscuit filled with bugs. And so great was the need that two dogs and two cats were eaten." These hardships, however, did not deter the Portuguese. Da Gama's stubborn determination fortified his men, and by the end of October 1503 all thirteen ships had reached the Tagus. D. Vasco arrived aboard the *São Jeronimo* with eight others on the tenth of that month. The fleet carried an incredibly rich cargo of between 30,000 and 35,000 *quintals* of spices, with perhaps 75% of it pepper. Once again, da Gama had more than justified his selection to lead an important expedition for the Crown. Yet, the decisive question in the fall of 1503 remained much the same as in 1499: How would both D. Manuel and D. Vasco seek to exploit these great successes?

The Good Life: Family and Fortune in Portugal, 1504–1523

"Admiral, friend. It seems to us that this petition that you present for the title of Count, which you say we had promised you, you have presented it as you saw fit, and we, on account of the services that you have done for us do not wish to give you the permission that you ask from us for you to leave our Kingdoms." D. Manuel I to D. Vasco da Gama, August 27, 1518

Summary

The chapter details Vasco da Gama's return to Lisbon after his second voyage and the additional rewards he received from D. Manuel. The creation of the Portuguese empire in Asia during the first two decades of the sixteenth century is described, along with the careers of D. Francisco de Almeida and Afonso de Albuquerque. The process by which Vasco da Gama successfully lobbied for the title of count and his influence at court is examined. The chapter concludes with the state of affairs in Portugal and her Asian possessions at the death of D. Manuel I in 1521 and the challenges confronting his son, D. João III.

Da Gama's Reception in Lisbon

When news reached the court that da Gama had returned "with very great wealth," D. Manuel I sent the captain of his guard,

D. Nuno Manuel, to greet D. Vasco and to conduct him to the Cathedral of Lisbon. According to Correia, D. Manuel then "went on horseback with many people to the cathedral, to give much praise to the Lord before the altar of Saint Vincent." After receiving the compliments of D. Nuno, da Gama and his captains disembarked and "coming out upon the shore they found many relations and friends, and horses, upon which they all mounted, and went their way to the cathedral, where the King ordered them to go and give praise to the Lord." After being met by several dignitaries, D. Vasco and his captains said their prayers and then made their way to D. Manuel in order to kiss his hand in a sign of fealty. The Portuguese king received D. Vasco and his men "with much honor, and with great rejoicings he mounted his horse, and went conversing with the Captain-major to the palace . . . [where] they went in to the Queen, and all of them kissed her hand and that of the Prince, the Queen showing them much honor." According to Barros, da Gama presented his monarch with a large silver basin containing the 500 *misqâls* in gold that had been rendered to D. Manuel as tribute by the sultan of Kilwa. In turn, D. Manuel ordered that a gold tabernacle be cast from this tribute which was presented to the church at Belém as a symbol of his initial successes in the Indian Ocean basin.

Relations Between D. Vasco and D. Manuel

Da Gama spent the next two decades living in Portugal, dividing his time between Lisbon and the Alentejo. Given this fact, it is perhaps surprising that the same lack of sources that characterized the initial decades of his life continued for these years as well. One issue to address for this period is the nature of the relationship between D. Vasco and D. Manuel. Both men possessed strong and somewhat mercurial personalities. Moreover, D. Manuel would not grant da Gama everything he promised him, while da Gama was impatient and sometimes too aggressive in his demands. As a result, periodic clashes between the two men occurred. Nevertheless, both men recognized the value and importance of the other to their goals. Da Gama had discovered the sea route to India and had begun to carve out a political, economic, and religious empire for D. Manuel in Asia, while only the king could elevate da Gama and his family to the upper echelons of the nobility in Portugal and all that elevation embodied. Neither would jeopardize this fundamental reality with a definitive break. During these decades, da Gama was busy and quite content solidifying the economic and social advancement that he had obtained in the wake of his first two voyages to India. He involved himself in court life and events in Asia according to his own desires and priorities. At the same time, D. Manuel solidified the foundation for an Asian empire that da Gama had laid. These parallel activities strengthened the bond between the two men, thus preventing a definitive rupture.

According to Correia, "To Dom Vasco he gave great favors, and all his goods free and exempt, and he granted him the anchorage dues of India, and made him admiral of its seas forever; and he bestowed the anchorage dues on his heirs." Correia's version also attests to da Gama's rise within the noble hierarchy at court in the years following 1504: "[D. Manuel] made him one of the principal men of his kingdom, and always increased him with greater honors, as will be seen further on in these histories." Da Gama also played a key role in the Crown's decisions relating to India in the years immediately following his second return from India. In 1505, following the original appointment of Tristão da Cunha to govern India for the following three years, a large fleet and orders were prepared, "with much assistance of Dom Vasco da Gama, who was the principal person in all the affairs of India." Later that year, D. Francisco de Almeida in fact sailed to India as Viceroy in place of da Cunha, whose temporary blindness had deprived him of this post. His fleet was prepared "according to the very full minutes which D. Vasco da Gama gave with respect to all, for he directed and ordained everything." The Viceroy spent much time during these preparations with da Gama, who thus exerted a powerful influence in the geopolitical and religious calculations of Almeida in this crucial phase of Portuguese empire building in Asia.

Da Gama's Life in Portugal, ca. 1503–1507

With the exception of Gaspar Correia's information, not much else is known of the exact movements or activities of da Gama from October 1503 until March 1507. D. Manuel continued to reward D. Vasco. On February 20, 1504, for example, he received a grant of 400,000 *reais* annually drawn from the salt tax of Lisbon to thank him for arranging the tribute from the sultan of Kilwa. That same month, the king's factor for Guinea and India began paying da Gama the 1000 *cruzados* that the king had earlier granted him, based on each caravel that came from São Jorge da Mina. Between November 1504 and July 1506, da Gama received 292,500 *reais* from this grant. Whether D. Manuel was sufficiently generous in these grants and how gracious da Gama was in receiving this largesse is difficult to determine. The Venetian Lunardo Ca Masser, resident in Lisbon in 1506, wrote that D. Vasco was not "very grateful to His Highness," and that in his actions at court he was "an intemperate man, without any reason." Yet, Ca Masser may have merely been seeking to fuel unrealistic hope of a split between D. Manuel and the most important man in the kingdom for Asian affairs. After all, at the time, his patrons in Italy had a powerful thirst for any news that might offer them hope in undermining the developing spice trade of their Iberian rivals.

The Dispute Over the Lordship of Sines, Again

Perhaps the most highly debated event during these years relates to Vasco da Gama's attempt to take up his grant of Sines. He had been granted lordship of the town in December 1499, but compensation to D. Jorge and the Order of Santiago had been difficult to arrange, and the transfer had languished. Perhaps emboldened by the success of his 1502 voyage, his position at court, and D. Manuel's continued favor, da Gama decided to stake his claim to Sines in an aggressive manner. Sometime between 1504 and 1506, D. Vasco moved his family to the town, began to construct his manor house, and began to comport himself like the Lord of the place. Whether he had been encouraged in these actions by anyone at court, or whether he expected any support for them, is unclear. What is certain is that D. Jorge complained to D. Manuel concerning these actions, and the king was obliged to rebuke his Admiral, at least formally, for them. On March 21, 1507, he issued a decree that ordered da Gama and his family to leave the town

Views of Church and Monastery of Jeronimos, Belem. (Glenn J. Ames)

within thirty days. D. Manuel forbade their return without the permission of the Master of Santiago, "my well-beloved and prized nephew," with the penalty of a 500-*cruzado* fine and the usual punishment "due to those who do not obey the command of their king and lord." The decree also ordered the cession of any building projects D. Vasco had begun, including the hermitage of São Giraldo and the church Nossa Senhora das Salas.

Complicating the task of sorting out this dispute is the fact that sometime before early June 1507, D. Vasco left the Order of Santiago for the Order of Christ. This action mimicked that of other nobles like D. Francisco de Almeida. Yet, the exact timing of this shift is crucial regarding the dispute over Sines. Da Gama may have threatened to resign from Santiago unless D. Jorge approved the transfer of the town and, when the Master refused, he decided to abandon the Order and hope for the intervention of the king regarding Sines. For political and social reasons, he may have already abandoned Santiago and in retaliation invited the protest of D. Jorge regarding Sines. Or in retaliation for D. Jorge's protest and his rebuke by D. Manuel in the spring of 1507, he may have abandoned Santiago in favor of the Order of Christ. Unfortunately, because we do not know the exact date of his shift in allegiance, the definitive story of the imbroglio over Sines cannot be resolved. In any event, D. Vasco and his family complied with the king's order and moved to Évora, which became the locus for their activities for the next dozen years.

Building a Portuguese Empire in Asia, 1503–1520

While Vasco da Gama was busy consolidating his royal grants and his family life in Portugal, the Crown continued its efforts to build upon his work in Asia and create a trading empire. In this impressive enterprise, D. Manuel confronted a daunting strategic and logistical challenge in constructing a viable military, administrative, economic, and religious presence thousands of miles from home in the face of stern and entrenched opposition. While periodic disputes arose on the Council regarding specific policies, there can be little doubt that the Portuguese hierarchy in general firmly supported this enterprise, an enterprise that promised lavish rewards for nearly all segments of society. Following da Gama's departure from India in February 1503, Vicente Sodré and his brother Braz Sodré embarked on a voyage to the Red Sea and Persian Gulf to disrupt Arab shipping with Kerala, to continue the struggle against Islam, and to get rich by capturing as many prizes as possible.

Some contemporaries criticized this action, arguing that it left the fledgling Portuguese posts at Cochin and Cannanur at great risk, given the likely aggression of a vengeful Samudri of Calicut. Nevertheless, the Sodré brothers demonstrated that Portuguese naval power would be felt not only along the western coast of India but in Arabian waters as well. As the Arabian chronicler Muhammad bin Umar al-Taiyab Ba Faqih noted: "In this year (Rajab 908/1503) the vessels of the Frank appeared at sea en route for India, Hurmuz, and those parts. They took about seven vessels, killing those on board and making some prisoner. This was their first action, may God curse them."

Although a storm battered the Portuguese fleet and both Sodré brothers perished, Pêro de Ataíde brought three of the ships back to India in the late summer of 1503. This voyage did not adversely affect the Cannanur factory, thanks to the deft actions of Gonçalo Gil Barbosa and his nephew Duarte Barbosa. However, the Samudri attacked Cochin, and the Portuguese factors there fled the city for a time with the Unni Goda Varma.

This temporary setback was overcome beginning in August 1503, as Portuguese naval power on the Malabar Coast became more entrenched during the remainder of that decade. First, Ataíde returned with the remnants of Vicente Sodré's fleet, and **Francisco de Albuquerque** arrived with a squadron of three ships, which had departed from Lisbon in April. Together, they forced the Samudri to withdraw, and Albuquerque soon constructed a strong wooden fortress in Cochin. The Portuguese position was further reinforced with the arrival in September of another three ships under the command of Francisco de Albuquerque's cousin, Afonso de Albuquerque. Confronted with this growing naval and military might, the Samudri signed a truce in December 1503. Nevertheless, the Samudri found a pretext to break this agreement soon thereafter and attacked Cochin once again with a large force.

It was certainly no coincidence that this renewed warfare followed the departure of the spice-laden fleets of Afonso and Francisco Albuquerque for Lisbon in early 1504. Only the skillful campaign waged by Duarte Pereira Pacheco, who remained in Cochin to command a garrison of approximately 100 Portuguese, 300 indigenous troops, and a handful of ships, managed to hold the Samudri at bay. Pacheco's garrison was only relieved with the arrival of a fourteen-ship fleet under Lopo Soares de Albergaria, which had departed Lisbon in April 1504 and reached India in September. D. Vasco advised D. Manuel that it was imperative to send out as many forces as possible at this crucial juncture in order to solidify the gains he had already made. The king, sensing greatness within his grasp, responded by furnishing Lopo Soares with some of the largest and most powerful ships he possessed. More than a thousand men embarked on these ships.

The Portuguese, much to the chagrin of the Samudri and his Muslim allies, were determined to remain in India. To prevent this unwelcome development, the adherents of Islam sought to mount an effective and swift counterattack. By 1505, rumors had already reached Cairo that the Iberians would soon attack Jiddah, the port for the holy city of Mecca. In November of that year **Emir Hussain Mushrif al-Kurdi** was sent from Cairo to the Red Sea to prevent such an attack. Overall, however, the response of the Islamic powers to the rapidly escalating Portuguese presence in the Indian Ocean trade was somewhat lethargic.

This lethargy was due in part to a succession struggle in Egypt at the end of the reign of Sultan Qa'it Bay (r. 1468–1496), which was resolved only with the accession to power of the mercurial Qansawh al-Ghawri (r. 1501–1516). Christian pressure in the eastern Mediterranean was also a concern, as were the difficulties inherent in coordinating an effective response in Constantinople, Cairo, and in the Indian–Muslim sultanates. The Venetians, by downplaying Portuguese naval power, also contributed to these delays. Finally, in the late summer of 1507, a Muslim champion set out to engage the unwanted Christians ("Franks"), who had already shown themselves to be little more than uncouth corsairs. Emir Hussain sailed out of the Red Sea in August or September of that year with a fleet of at least twelve ships and 1500 men-at-arms to defend Muslim dominance over the Indian Ocean trade. According to the Arab sources, he was a "holy warrior" (mujâhid fi sabil Allah) sent "to engage the Franks who had appeared in the Ocean and cut the Muslim trade routes."

D. Francisco de Almeida Appointed the First Viceroy of Portuguese Asia

By that time D. Manuel, once again acting on the advice of Vasco da Gama, had decided to appoint a Viceroy for his Asian possessions. This most important Crown official would govern for three years and ideally bring order, continuity, and structure to what had hitherto been a de facto empire. After the temporary blindness of Tristão da Cunha had disqualified him from this office, the king turned to the well-connected and powerful nobleman D. Francisco de Almeida, a son of the first count of Abrantes. Both Almeida's fleet and his instructions were prepared in close consultation with D. Vasco. Ultimately, Almeida's fleet comprised some twenty-two ships and over 2500 men, including 1500 men-at-arms. Ideally, half of these ships were to return to Portugal with cargoes, while the rest would remain in Asia to protect the king's settlements. After capturing Kilwa Kisiwani and building a strong fort there in July 1505, Almeida then reduced Mombasa before heading for India. Following his instructions, the Viceroy then fortified the Portuguese on Anjedive Island near Goa, at Cannanur, and finally at Cochin, where he established his headquarters.

During the next three years, Almeida did much to entrench Portuguese power in the Indian Ocean spice trade. He signed an advantageous commercial treaty with the sultan of Melaka, an important entrepôt for the Indonesian and South China Sea trade. His son, **D. Lourenço de Almeida**, began the process of opening up a trade for cinnamon on the island of Ceylon. D. Manuel's first Viceroy had also been instructed to formalize a pass, or *cartaz*, system whereby indigenous captains would have to procure signed passes from the Portuguese in order to pursue a trade in the Indian Ocean. Armed fleets would patrol the main shipping routes, and ships without such a pass were fair prizes for the Portuguese.

By 1508, the Portuguese were clearly gaining the upper hand in their struggle with the various Muslim powers in the trade. Between 1497 and 1500, the Crown had sent some seventeen ships to India. From 1501 until 1510, more than 150 ships left Lisbon for the Indian Ocean. In terms of tonnage, the figures climbed from 2,665 tons to 42,775 tons. The Portuguese also sent larger cargoes of spices back to Lisbon. The fleet of 1505 returning under Lopo Soares de Albergaria, for example, carried more than 1,121,000 kgs. in spices and other goods, including over 1,000,000 kgs. in pepper. The Portuguese also effectively shut off the traditional flow of spices through the Levant, which had previously made the Italians, and particularly the Venetians, rich. At Alexandria, for example, the average annual cargo in pepper had ranged from between 480 and 630 tons from 1496 to 1498. That figure had dropped to only 135 tons for the years 1501–1506. At Beruit, the story was much the same. For these same years, the average amount of pepper had fallen from anywhere between 90 to 240 tons to only 10 tons.

The Muslim Response: Triumph and Tragedy

To reverse this disturbing trend for Islam, Emir Hussain Mushrif al-Kurdi's powerful fleet reached the Indian coast in late 1507. Malik Ayaz, the governor of Diu for Sultan Mahmud of Gujarat, also provided some sixty small ships for the Muslim armada. In March 1508, the youthful D. Lourenço de Almeida was patrolling this coast in search of prizes and to protect Portuguese trade. Near the port of Chaul, the Viceroy's son engaged this powerful fleet with a force of twelve ships and 600 men. In a three-day battle, the superiority of Portuguese shipborne artillery might have been reconfirmed. But the overwhelming numbers of Amir Husain and Malik Ayaz and tactical mistakes on the part of D. Lourenço resulted in the defeat of the Portuguese. D. Lourenço's flagship was eventually captured, with only nineteen of its crew still alive. During the final stages of the battle, D. Lourenço had himself tied to the mast, after having his thigh broken by a ball, in order to lead his men. There, he was struck in the back by another ball and killed. In this engagement, the Portuguese lost 140 men and had 124 wounded. The Muslim losses were perhaps 400. News of Emir Hussain's victory in this battle touched off three days of celebration in Cairo. Yet these celebrations were premature.

The death of his beloved son only hardened Almeida's antipathy toward Islam. **Afonso de Albuquerque** reached Cochin in late 1508 with secret orders from the king naming him Governor of Portuguese India. Yet, Almeida refused to hand over power to his successor until he had exacted revenge against Emir Hussain and Malik Ayaz. The Viceroy sailed north on December 12, 1508, with eighteen ships and 1200 men. On February 2, 1509, the fleet reached the Gujarati city of Diu. There, Emir Hussain's fleet of 12 Egyptian ships, supported by perhaps another 100 Muslim ships, waited at anchor. On February 3, in one of the seminal naval battles of the sixteenth century, the Portuguese Viceroy advanced into the harbor and engaged the Muslim fleet. In this fierce battle, Almeida's triumph was complete. Emir Hussain was wounded, and his fleet was badly mauled in the all-day encounter. Most of the Muslim ships were plundered and then set aflame. The flags of the Sultan of Egypt and Emir Hussain were both captured and sent to Lisbon. More importantly, Muslim naval power in the Indian Ocean was destroyed, thus opening even greater possibilities for Portuguese pretensions in Asia. Almeida then arranged from a cowered Malik Ayaz for the release of the surviving seventeen Portuguese prisoners taken at Chaul. On his return voyage to Cochin, Almeida demonstrated his naval power by forcing Chaul to pay tribute. According to one source, the Viceroy also executed some of his captives on this voyage south and then fired their limbs toward the main Muslim towns he passed in a more gruesome demonstration of revenge for his son.

Afonso de Albuquerque and the Consolidation of Empire, 1509–1515

The superiority of Portuguese naval power and the foundations of a trading empire in Asia were confirmed during the Governorship of Afonso de Albuquerque, who finally took power from Almeida in November 1509. Albuquerque, like Vasco da Gama, was single-minded and relentless in his quest for Portuguese power in the Indian Ocean. Albuquerque was extremely well educated, and his letters to D. Manuel reveal brilliance of language and strategy that remain unsurpassed in the annals of the European quest for empire in Asia. Albuquerque's strategy for commercial dominance called for the Portuguese to control key points on the traditional trading routes in the Indian Ocean. These points included strategic cities near the mouth of the Persian Gulf and Red Sea, the traditional routes for the caravan trade to Europe, as well as a position at the nexus of the Indonesian and Malaysian trades, and a base in India. Strong fortresses would be established at these points, with surrounding territory to provide greater security. In turn, these fortresses would serve as the loci for Portuguese fleets sent out to enforce the *cartaz* system, as well as providing collection and embarkation points for the trade with Europe and elsewhere. Obviously, this aggressive and dynamic strategy not only involved a sizable investment on the part of the Crown, it also engendered a good deal of debate and, at times, jealously in both Lisbon and Cochin. Albuquerque, however, in serving the Crown in Africa and on his initial voyage to India in 1503–1504 had already demonstrated a strength of character that would sustain him through these challenges.

Albuquerque began his second voyage to India in April 1506, commanding five ships in the sixteen-ship fleet under Tristão da Cunha. After bombarding several cities along the East African coast and reinforcing a fortress on the island of Socotra, Albuquerque separated from da Cunha. He attacked and sacked several towns along the Omani coast, cutting the ears and noses off the inhabitants who betrayed him. Albuquerque then began to implement his strategy to dominate the trade between Europe and Asia by capturing the rich entrepôt of Hurmuz at the mouth of the Persian Gulf.

Albuquerque and his small squadron reached India in December 1508. There, his dispute with Almeida over relinquishing power to him had dragged on for nearly a year. Only the arrival of the Marshall of Portugal, D. Fernando Coutinho, with a fleet of eighteen ships and 1600 soldiers, in late October 1509 broke this stalemate. Coutinho, a relative of Albuquerque, carried orders reconfirming his succession as Governor. The Marshall had also been instructed by D. Manuel to use this force to destroy the power of the Samudri of Calicut, a goal that was no doubt strongly endorsed by Vasco da Gama. In Cochin, Coutinho ensured that Albuquerque took power as Captain-general and Governor of India in early November. Yet, the limitations of Coutinho as a warrior were soon revealed in his bungled sack of Calicut in early January 1510. Coutinho, who ignored Albuquerque's advice several times during this attack, spent much more time and energy setting fire to a mosque and to the palace of the Samudri than in defeating the troops of his enemy. This tactical mistake cost Coutinho his life during a wild retreat to the beach. Albuquerque received two wounds in the shoulder as well. But at least he now had a free hand to implement his grand plans for further establishing Portuguese geopolitical, religious, and economic power in the Indian Ocean basin, assisted by a large fleet of twenty-three ships.

The new Governor had originally prepared an expedition for the Red Sea. But, on the persuasive advice of the Hindu corsair Timoja, he instead turned his attention to the port of Goa on the Konkan coast. This rich city was then under the control of the Muslim Adil Shah dynasty of Bijapur. Albuquerque captured Goa in March 1510. In May, he was forced to abandon the city when the king of Bijapur, **Yusuf Adil Shah,** launched a spirited counterattack. After supporting the king of Cochin against the Samudri in September 1510, Albuquerque returned north and definitively

Map of Goa, ca. 1650? From *Asia Portuguesa Tomo I de Manuel de Faria Sousa*, Lisbon, 1666. (Glenn J. Ames)

recaptured Goa on St. Catherine's Day (November 25) 1510. As he informed D. Manuel in a letter in December: "In the capture of Goa the Turks lost over 300 men . . . Many were also drowned whilst crossing the river. I afterwards sacked the city in which for four days the carnage was fearful, as no quarter was given to anyone. The agricultural laborers and the Hindus were spared, but of the Moors killed the number was at least 6000. It was indeed a great deed, and well carried out."

The capture of Goa by Albuquerque provided a strategically located capital for the *Estado da India* for the next four centuries. To provide the Portuguese with a base to influence the rich Malaysian and Indonesian trade, Albuquerque then captured and fortified the notable entrepôt of Melaka in August 1511. On his return voyage to India, his flagship, the *Flor de la Mar*, was shipwrecked, and the Governor barely survived. Reaching Goa in September 1512, he repulsed another Bijapuri attack and then prepared an expedition to capture the town of Aden near the mouth of the Red Sea. Yet, his attack on Aden, launched in March 1513, failed. Albuquerque partially atoned for this setback in May 1515 when he again captured Hurmuz, a vital possession, in particular for the lucrative horse trade with India. The Portuguese Crown would control Hurmuz until 1622. The difficult climate and the work required to fortify this valued conquest, however, took a toll on Albuquerque's health. Nevertheless, he completed the fortress there before sailing for Goa. Albuquerque died aboard the *Flor da Rosa* in sight of his Asian capital on December 16, 1515, having established the basis for Portuguese dominance over the European share of the Indian Ocean trade for the next century. As he informed D. Manuel: "Sire, I do not write to your Highness in my own hand because it trembles greatly when I do so, and this forecasts death . . . As for the affairs of India . . . everything is settled."

Da Gama's Life in Portugal, 1507–1523

Vasco da Gama followed these events with a good deal of interest from his house in Évora. To remind him of the source of his newfound wealth, the Admiral had ordered frescos painted in the courtyard of his home depicting fauna, real and mythical, and flora relating to the voyage to India. D. Vasco continued to receive royal favor from his monarch throughout these years, and D. Manuel's decree of March 1507 should not be seen as proof of a serious conflict between them. The king soon thereafter granted da Gama the rights to additional royal revenues in Sines and surrounding towns. All of these places were located in the territory of the Order of Santiago, a fact surely not lost on D. Jorge and the hierarchy of the Order. The king also took an interest in ensuring that D. Vasco received these revenues. On November 19, 1511, D. Manuel ordered relevant local officials to collect these monies fairly and to make them available promptly to the agents of the Admiral. This grant not only maintained the traditional links of da Gama to the region around Sines dominated by Santiago, but it also tempered the order of expulsion from Sines.

In June 1513, to reward his services, the king exempted any permissible products that da Gama imported from India from duty or freight charges. In the summer of 1515, he bequeathed rights to hunt in the royal preserves at Niza and authorized D. Vasco to send an agent paid by the Crown aboard all fleets sent to India to negotiate business for him. In October 1515, D. Manuel also conferred an annual pension of 60,000 *reais* for his office of Admiral of the India Sea. Another grant of this same month exempted D. Vasco "and all members of his house" from paying real estate or excise taxes wherever he should reside or own property. Da Gama, moreover, maintained at least indirect links with the Order of Santiago even after his shift of allegiance. His sister, Teresa, married Lope Mendes de Vasconcelos, whose grandfather had been Master of the Order and who had strong ties with Santiago. This marriage yielded her an annual pension of 20,000 *reais* from D. Manuel.

During his twelve years in Évora, D. Vasco traveled to court, to Lisbon, and to the estates of family and friends. He also purchased or leased properties in Lisbon and in the area around Portalegre and Niza close to the border with Spain. In December of either 1514 or 1515 D. Vasco wrote a letter to Antonio Carneiro, secretary to D. Manuel, seeking assistance for three of his minions who had been accused of poaching (killing a boar) on the royal reserves in Niza. "My Lord: Antonio Lopes and Fernand Anes and Francysco Anes, squires resident in Benevente are men for whom I desire to do a great deal." Da Gama asked that Carneiro "get an order signed by His Highness in which he lets them go free, and they give over 100 *cruzado*s each in bond," and if he could "you my lord would do me a great favor." In July 1518, D. Vasco spent time in Lisbon and assisted his younger brother, D. Aires da Gama, in receiving the final third (ca. 117,000 *reais*) of his sister-in-law's dowry from the Crown. The documentation on this matter was written "in the houses of the residence of the lord Admiral, D. Vasco da Gama" in Lisbon. That same month, da Gama attended the marriage ceremony of D. Manuel to Dona Leonora, the sister of Charles V.

Da Gama Presses for the Title of Count

In 1518, D. Vasco pressed his claim to the title of count. This elevation to the ranks of the *titulares* (titled ones) had evidently been promised to him in return for his services to the Crown, but it had not been forthcoming. The Admiral took an aggressive stance in this matter, although the question of just how aggressive is impossible to gauge given the lack of his formal petition to D. Manuel. Nevertheless, D. Vasco evidently asked that the title be granted immediately; if not, he sought the king's permission to leave Portugal and offer his services to another king. The timing of this petition suggests that D. Vasco sought to force the king's hand by exploiting the case of **Fernão de Magalhaes** (Ferdinand Magellan). Magalhaes had an impressive record serving D. Manuel in Asia from 1505–1513. He had fought in East Africa and on the Malabar coast of India with Almeida. Under Albuquerque, he had taken part in the capture of both Goa and Melaka. After returning to Lisbon, however, at least two of his petitions for rewards were rejected by D. Manuel. In October 1517 he left Portugal and traveled to Spain. By 1518, Magellan had signed an agreement with Charles V, which promised considerable rewards in return for establishing the Spanish Crown in the spice-rich Molucca Islands. The threat in D. Vasco's petition was that if his request were not granted, he too would offer his services to D. Manuel's brother-in-law and great rival.

In August 1518, D. Manuel responded to this petition but avoided a direct response on the issue of granting the title of count. "Admiral, friend. It seems to us that this petition that you present to us for the title of Count, which you say we had promised you, you have presented it as you saw fit." Unfortunately, D. Manuel did not provide any insights as to whether he had promised the title or not. As for the request to leave the kingdom, the king noted: "we, on account of the services that you have done us do not wish to give you the permission that you ask from us for you to leave our Kingdoms, but by this, we order that you remain in our Kingdoms until the end of the month of December." D. Manuel, by ordering da Gama to remain in Portugal for the remainder of the year, was hoping that he would "see the error" he was committing. If, after that time, the Admiral felt the same "even though we would feel this heavily, we would not prevent you from going or from taking your wife and children and your moveable goods" and leaving the kingdom. Privately, the king was probably stung by da Gama's request. Of course, D. Vasco forced the king to reevaluate his stance on the issue of raising him to the ranks of the *titulares*. This was a weighty decision, a move that would complete the rise of D. Vasco and his family from its relatively humble provincial roots to the elite of noble society. There were less than twenty titled noblemen in the entire kingdom in 1521, ten of them counts. This was a crucial step in the history of any noble family, and it was obviously a promotion that da Gama believed was worth risking a great deal to attain.

In the end, D. Vasco won this high-stakes game. D. Jaime, duke of Braganza and a nephew of D. Manuel, offered to surrender the town of Vidigueira to D. Vasco in return for certain considerations. On October 24, 1519, D. Manuel sanctioned this deal, and the formal documents were signed on November 4. D. Jaime agreed to hand over the towns of Vidigueira and Villa de Frade to D. Vasco da Gama, who in turn signed over his hereditary pension from the king of 1000 *cruzado*s and a one-time cash payment of 4000 *cruzado*s in gold. This transaction was signed at Évora on November 7, 1519. On this document D. Vasco's wife's name appears in full for the first time. D. Manuel made the deal irrevocable for all time "in virtue of the many and important services which we have received from the said admiral, especially in the discovery of the Indies, which have redounded and redound to the Crown of our kingdom, and in general to its inhabitants and to those of all Christianity." On December 29, 1519, a legal representative of D. Vasco, Estêvão Lopes, formally took possession of Vidigueira. That same day, in Évora, D. Manuel formally conferred "the title of Count of the city of Vidigueira, and we create him Count with all the prerogatives, and franchises enjoyed by the Counts of the kingdom by virtue of the very great and signal service which Vasco da Gama performed in the discovery of the Indies." So, within six months of receiving D. Manuel's letter forbidding him to leave the kingdom, D. Vasco had entered senhorial society in Portugal, obtaining a coveted title and seignory in the process. Perhaps the only bittersweet aspect of the events of late 1519 for da Gama was that he had not won the lordship of Sines, which he had desired since at least 1499.

Da Gama Takes Up Residence in Vidigueira

Vasco da Gama and his family moved to Vidigueira in 1520. The new count spent the next four years settling himself there. All of the leading nobles and civil officials of Vidigueira and Vila de Frades attended the transfer ceremonies. Both the local elite and populace welcomed D. Vasco with open arms. After all, the transfer brought advantages to all. Da Gama became a count and member of the noble elite thanks to Vidigueira. This modest Alentejo town, which was a backwater in the plethora of possessions of the duke of Braganza, had been elevated to the seat of a county, a fact that gave its name a new prestige in the kingdom. D. Vasco, his wife "the magnificent lady Dona Catarina de Átaide, *almiranta*," and children took possession of the castle of the town and used it as their formal residence or manor house. In truth, this edifice was not really an authentic fortress in the medieval sense but more of a palace with fortifications. The family crest adorns the ruins of the castle of Vidigueira to this day.

In Vidigueira, da Gama found a tranquil and agreeable home. He spent much of his time overseeing the management of

Frescos of Flora and Fauna of India, Da Gama's House, Évora.
(Glenn J. Ames)

his new domains. The count also sought to ingratiate himself with the local population. In 1520, for example, he paid for a bell to be cast for the town's clock tower, or *Torre do Relógio*. Along the base of the bell, the inscription in Gothic script reads: "This bell the Count Dom Vasco Admiral of India caused to be cast in the year 1520." On one side is a relief of the cross of the Order of Christ, and on the other, the coat of arms of the da Gama family. Local folklore holds that the metal for this bell was taken from one of the cannon from his first expedition to India. Another story holds that the bell came from the ship *São Gabriel* from the epic voyage of 1497. Both stories are apocryphal. D. Vasco and Dona Catarina also showed great interest in the nearby Convent and Church of Nossa Senhora das Relíquias (Our Lady of the Relics). They endowed a chapel in the church and arranged for their remains to be interred there after their deaths.

Prosperity for Da Gama and Portugal

The early 1520s was a period of great prosperity for Vasco da Gama, for Portugal, and for her Asian empire. Lisbon was the greatest commercial center in Europe, with great wealth from the African and Indian trades pouring into the royal coffers of D. Manuel. The great monastery and church at Belém were fitting monuments to this golden age of Portuguese expansion and power. Similarly, Albuquerque's conquest, Goa, remained one of the richest and most desired cities in the overseas empires of the European powers. Goa served as the terminus of the lucrative horse trade from Persia to India. Gold, ivory, and slaves came in from East Africa in return for Indian cotton cloth. Spices from the Malabar coast and the Moluccas also flowed to the Portuguese Asian capital. Precious gems, cinnamon, and pearls were sent there from Ceylon. Goa also served as the seat of administration for the *Estado da India*, with the Viceroy or Governor overseeing the political, diplomatic, and economic structures of the empire from the Konkan coast, centrally located within the Indian Ocean basin. The first priests had come out with the fleets of da Gama, Cabral, and others. A grateful Papacy bestowed a monopoly for spreading the

Catholic faith in Africa, Brazil, and Asia upon the Portuguese Crown in a series of bulls. These bulls made the king of Portugal the "standard bearer of the Faith" in those regions. These religious activities in Asia were eventually administered from Goa, which became the first bishopric in Asia in 1534 and archbishopric in 1560.

Death of D. Manuel I; the Reign of D. João III

Yet, things were not perfect. D. Vasco contented himself with Vidigueira, not Sines. Similarly, the process of overseas expansion that had largely dominated the interests and resources of the Crown since ca. 1420 probably retarded agricultural developments and drained excessive manpower from the relatively small kingdom. Moreover, Albuquerque's successors had not followed his example, or that of D. Vasco, with respect to enriching oneself at Crown expense in Asia. Lopo Soares de Albergaria (1515–1518) allowed his associates to exploit the trade for private gain and undertook an ill-fated expedition to the Red Sea. Diogo Lopes de Sequeira (1518–1522) attempted to reduce Diu but accomplished little during his tenure, save for lining his own pockets. **D. Duarte de Menezes** (1522–24) was "a thoroughgoing rascal, licentious and greedy even for his time." He did at least find the tomb of the Apostle St. Thomas, who had been martyred in India centuries before. Nevertheless, despite these problems, D. Vasco had attained wealth and fame and entered the upper echelons of Portuguese society; Portugal had entered the ranks of the leading powers in Europe; and the *Estado da India* remained the most formidable power, both economically and militarily, in the Indian Ocean.

At the end of 1521, an epidemic swept through Portugal, and even "Manuel the Fortunate" could not escape its grasp. As Damião de Góis wrote, the king "rendered up his soul to his creator, on the ninth day of his illness, in his palace in Lisbon 13 December." As Góis described the king: "He was the first European monarch to possess elephants, brought from India, and once had paraded through the city a rhinoceros and a panther, gifts from the king of Hurmuz." As for his personal habits, "he was chaste, clean in person and well dressed, wearing something new nearly every day . . . He was a good business-man, and worked quickly. He was temperate in eating and drank only water . . . He was a good and strict Catholic." But now he was dead and soon buried fittingly at the Monastery of Jeronimos at Belém.

The throne, at this crucial moment, passed to his eldest son, then nineteen years old, who took the title **D. João III**. The new king took possession of the Crown with much ceremony. The chronicler, Garcia de Resende, who lived through three reigns, wrote that he had never seen such pomp. The "King of the world appeared in power and in perfection." D. João "rode to his coronation mounted on a handsome gray horse. He was clad in a long brocade robe, with a long train lined with the fur of martens." In the procession, he was preceded "by a prince of the blood royal, bearing in his hands the baton of a marshal, while John's bridle was held by another royal prince." Included among these leading nobles of the kingdom escorting the new king was "the illustrious Count of Vidigueira, Dom Vasco da Gama."

D. Vasco's role in the coronation ceremony reflected the degree to which he had risen within the ruling elite of Portugal since his early days in Sines or even in 1499. In 1522 and 1523, the young king confirmed all of the grants that his father had bestowed upon him. Additionally, in March 1522, D. João also conceded to da Gama the revenues from the anchorage fees of Goa, Melaka, and Hurmuz. The young king would also end the count's peaceful sojourn in Vidigueira. After two decades removed from the fields of conquest in India, D. João III selected da Gama to return there in 1524 and named him as only the second Viceroy in the history of the *Estado da India*. The young king and his council decided that the lack of firm direction in Portuguese Asia that had characterized the final years of D. Manuel's reign had to be corrected before serious problems developed in the empire. Clearly, only a firm man, much respected and indeed feared, possessing the requisite knowledge of Asia, and having a suitable social rank, would do for this title and mission. Of all the men in the kingdom, in fact, only D. Vasco da Gama possessed all of these qualities. The count was now well into his fifties. He had spent years of relative ease on his estates. Could he muster the will and energy to accomplish this final task for the Crown? That was undoubtedly the question on many minds in both Lisbon and Vidigueira in early 1524. Only time and a long ocean voyage would reveal the answer.

Views of Bell Tower and Bell donated by da Gama, ca. 1520, Vidigueira. (Glenn J. Ames)

VI

"Viceroy of India," 1524: The Culmination of a Life and a Career

"Friends! Rejoice and be joyful, for even the sea trembles before us!" D. Vasco da Gama to his crew off the Indian coast, September 1524

Summary

The chapter details the last year of Vasco da Gama's life and his final voyage to India in 1524. D. João III's reasons for selecting him as Viceroy and da Gama's reasons for accepting this position are explained. The administrative, economic, and military reforms in both Goa and Cochin that da Gama carried out are also described. Finally, Da Gama's power struggle with D. Duarte de Menezes is examined. The chapter concludes with his death in Cochin on Christmas Eve 1524.

Selection of D. Vasco da Gama As Viceroy of India, 1523–1524

On Christmas Eve of 1523 Vasco da Gama enjoyed the considerable benefits and wealth that had come to him and his family thanks to his services to the Crown. The count of Vidigueira probably passed this special holiday season comfortably ensconced in his manor house, surrounded by family and friends in the midst of the rural Alentejo. Christmas Eve of 1524, however, found him thousands of miles from home, lying on his

127

deathbed on the Malabar coast of India in the midst of an important campaign to correct the worrying abuses that had crept into the imperial system in Asia. How had this stark shift occurred?

As early as the summer of 1523, the young king had considered naming D. Vasco to this position. According to his chronicler, Francisco de Andrada, the king "determined to send a man to govern there, through whom . . . India would perceive the great importance that was given to what was necessary for it and with whom His Highness would be sure not only that he would preserve what had been gained, but increase it as far as possible." The formal nomination for Viceroy was made after months of negotiation on January 26, 1524. A royal decree dated February 5 refers to D. Vasco as Viceroy of India. The terms of this *alvará* reflect some of the conditions the Admiral set forth before formally accepting this office and mission. In particular, D. João III guaranteed that in the event of da Gama's death, his eldest son, D. Francisco, would succeed to his title and estates without formalities or delays. On February 28, D. Vasco, in a formal ceremony in Évora, took an oath of fealty to the king and mission. He likely saw this enterprise as offering a fitting conclusion to his career and a demonstration of the considerable wealth and power he had obtained. Da Gama would also use this position to entrench his family more firmly into the sinews of the Asian empire of Portugal. His negotiations with D. João over the appointment not only yielded the title of Viceroy for himself, but also the captaincy of Melaka for his sons in succession and the title of Captain-major of the Indian Seas for his second son.

Da Gama's Fleet of 1524 and His Mission in India

The fleet of 1524 that formed in the Tagus well reflected the power that both the Portuguese Crown and D. Vasco had obtained thanks to the 1497 voyage and subsequent actions in the Indian Ocean basin. The new Viceroy sailed with fourteen ships: seven great ships, or *nao*s, three galleons, and four caravels. Correia described these ships as carrying "3000 men, many of them *fidalgos*, cavaliers, and men who had served in the household of the king, among them many of breeding and education." Supplementing these crews "was a reserve group to man the ships already stationed in the Indian Ocean." D. Vasco's eldest son, D. Francisco, was already assured, assuming he did not die, of inheriting his father's titles and estates. His father had, therefore, already handsomely provided for him. The Viceroy took two of his younger sons on this voyage: D. Estêvão, with the title Captain-major of the Indian Seas, and D. Paulo.

In an attempt to regularize the imperial succession in Goa, which, given the distances involved and high mortality rates, had been anything but efficient, D. Vasco carried three sealed letters. The first named the Viceroy's replacement in case of his death in office; the second, the successor's replacement in case of his death; and so on. These sealed letters were eventually held in a chest with three locks held by the *Vedor da Fazenda* in Goa, the second most powerful royal official in the *Estado da India*. Da Gama thus inaugurated a succession system that would endure for generations.

The fleet left Belém on April 9, 1524, but could not pass the bar at the mouth of the Tagus until April 16. Da Gama embarked aboard his flagship, the *St. Catherine of Mount Sinai*. Although it had been two decades since he had left the kingdom, D. Vasco quickly demonstrated that the years of aristocratic life had not softened him and that he had embraced D. João's mission of cleaning up abuses that had begun to infect Portugal's Asian empire. Even before leaving Belém, the Viceroy issued firm orders on one such abuse: women stowaways aboard ships sailing to India. Da Gama took this action "both for their [the women's] souls" and to avoid the quarrels and plots that resulted from this practice. His proclamation, barring this practice, was read to the crews on shore and posted on the foot of the masts. Any women found aboard ship "would be flogged publicly, even though she were married." Moreover, if she were married, "her husband would be sent back to Portugal in chains." If she were a captive or a slave, "she would be sold for the ransom of a captive." Finally, any captain who "found a woman on his ship and did not surrender her would lose his commission." The passage to Mozambique was relatively un-eventful. According to Barros, the fleet anchored there on August 14, in part so that D. Vasco could repair a yardarm. While there, three women who had either stowed away or had been smuggled aboard by the crews were handed over to him. The Viceroy had these women locked up until the fleet reached Goa.

Da Gama, like all good mariners on the sea route to India, well appreciated the necessity of a prompt departure from Mozambique and the African coast in order to benefit from the favorable winds of the southwest monsoon. He wanted, at all costs, to avoid "wintering" there. In fact, he did not even risk a stop at the traditionally friendly port of Malindi. The Admiral merely sent an envoy there "with letters of great friendship, and asking pardon for not going to him [the King of Malindi] in person, as he had a large fleet to lade and time was wanting." Although the Portuguese fleet caught the end of the monsoon winds, the journey up the east coast of Africa and across the Arabian Sea was problematic. At least four vessels were lost. The galleon of D. Fernando de Monroyo hit a reef off the coast of Malindi and floundered. Fortunately, its crew was saved. Scurvy also broke out. Finally, the crew of the caravel com-manded by Mossem Gaspar Malhorquim (from Majorca) mu-tinied, killed their captain, and began a pirating campaign near the Straits of Bab el Mandeb at the entrance of the Red Sea. This marauding only stopped in 1525, when Antonio Miranda d'Azevedo captured these men and brought them to Goa, where most of them were hanged.

By early September, D. Vasco and his ten remaining ships were just off the Indian coast near Dabul. At this point, an earthquake struck close to the Portuguese fleet. According to Correia's account, "the sea trembled in such manner, giving such great buffets to the ships, that all thought they were on the shoals, and struck the sails, and lowered the boats into the sea with great shouts and cries, and discharge of cannon." But when soundings were quickly taken, "they did not find any bot-tom, and they cried to God for mercy, because the ships pitched so violently that the men could not stand upright, and the chests were sent from one end of the ship to the other." These shocks "came on with violence, and died off, and then again were renewed, each time during the space of a Credo." Overall, "the whole lasted about an hour, in which the water made a great boiling up." In the midst of this chaos, D. Vasco calmly appeared with a physician and an astrologer who "at once said to the Viceroy that it was a quaking of the sea." In Barros's version, seeing the panic spreading among his crew, D. Vasco exclaimed: "Friends! Be glad and joyful, for the sea trembles at us: have no fear, for this is an earthquake." The only casualty from this bizarre episode was one member of the crew who had jumped overboard, thinking the flagship had struck a shoal. Once again, however, the Admiral had demonstrated self-assurance in the midst of great danger and the wisdom of his monarch in appointing him to such an important command.

Several days later, the fleet encountered a Muslim ship returning to India from Aden that had also weathered the effects of the earthquake. D. Jorge de Meneses's ship captured this vessel and declared it a legitimate prize. In an effort to regularize the enforcement of the lucrative *cartaz* system, D. Vasco had the confiscated cargo of this ship carefully recorded: 60,000 *cruzado*s in cash and goods worth another 200,000 *cruzados*. From the pilots of this Muslim ship, he also learned that Diu was three days away. Yet, it was not until September 15 that the newly fortified Portuguese fort at the port of Chaul was reached. There, at his first landfall in India, he began to use the title of Viceroy, as his orders from the king allowed.

At Chaul, D. Vasco began to implement his strategy for reining in the abuses that had crept into the imperial system in Asia. This strategy, as in his previous voyages, combined a firm hand for dealing with those who stepped beyond "the pale" of acceptable behavior while rewarding those who, like himself, had honorably served the Crown. Da Gama, as he probably recognized off Chaul, was the most compelling example of what such honorable service could bestow. The rather humble, poor provincial noble who had reached India in 1498 with three sparsely crewed ships had returned aboard a powerful fleet as Viceroy of an impressive string of fortresses, a count, propertied and rich beyond the imagination of most of his crew members.

Crime and corruption did indeed pay, but usually only in the short term. Crusading, fighting, killing, and trading for the Crown brought longer-lasting rewards for oneself and for one's family. This was the lesson of da Gama's life, and it was one that, if properly instructed, could easily stamp out the more worrying problems then affecting the *Estado da India*.

Problems in the Portuguese Indian Possessions

The situation in India upon the new Viceroy's arrival certainly called for some reforms. The Governor, D. Duarte de Menezes (1522–24), who arrived in Goa with his brother **D. Luiz de Menezes** in August 1521 and assumed power in January 1522, had inherited some worrying problems. Relations with Diu and Hurmuz in particular were volatile for the Crown. In fact, D. Duarte was attending to business in Hurmuz and the Persian Gulf region when D. Vasco arrived. Nevertheless, Menezes, who had built a reputation fighting the Muslims in North Africa, had not distinguished himself during his administration. His main objective was to accumulate wealth for himself, while administration and justice became lax and corrupt. Word of these problems reached Lisbon and, according to D. Vasco, Menezes had become "the scandal of Portugal."

As a result, D. Vasco sailed from Lisbon armed with a long, formal document titled "Articles for the investigation of D. Duarte, Captain of India." The charges in this document ranged from the general to the specific, encompassing financial, administrative, and even personal transgressions. It was alleged that D. Duarte had traded with the king's money, had taken for himself the estates and monies of deceased persons, had received bribes in judicial and administrative matters, had failed to favor Indian Christians, and had slept with married and non-Christian women. These misdeeds had forced many of the king's honest subjects to flee the *Estado da India*. In short, D. Duarte was accused of subverting the imperial system in almost every conceivable manner. Among the men who had returned to Lisbon and then denounced him was Garcia de Sá, who claimed that he had given the Governor a gold necklace and cup so as to be named captain of one of the ships returning to Lisbon. Several of the agents who D. Vasco had been sending to India to exploit and protect his royal grants regarding the trade had also furnished damning information on the Governor's shady dealings.

Da Gama's Reforms in India

As soon as the Viceroy reached Chaul, he began his reformation. In an effort to root out administrative corruption, both D. João III and D. Vasco had done their utmost to attract the very best of the Portuguese nobility to sail with the 1524 expedition. As Correia described, da Gama "brought with him very brilliant soldiery, and as captains, men of high family, the greater part of whom had been brought up in the labors of Indian affairs." Such men would replace those royal servants under the cloud of suspicion in Asia, especially those with close ties to Menezes. At Chaul, D. Duarte had replaced the able Henrique de Meneses with the rather unsavory Simão de Andrade, a close friend whose main qualification for the position was that he had married D. Duarte's illegitimate daughter. Because D. Vasco had given firm orders that no one was to land from the fleet, Andrade had gone aboard the *Saint Catherine of Mount Sinai*, and a council was held with the fleet's officers. At this meeting, the Viceroy replaced Andrade with one of the more suitable young nobles aboard the fleet, Christovão de Sousa, "according to instruction from the King." D. Vasco "also made appointments in all posts high and low, because he had instructions to make appointments for everything wherever he arrived." In this wholesale campaign of administrative reform, the Viceroy did not even have to wait for D. Duarte "to give in his accounts, since the King was very indignant with him for his evil deeds." D. Vasco then left firm written instructions for the new Captain to ignore any commands D. Duarte might seek to give if he appeared. Several days later the fleet headed south.

On September 23, 1524, D. Vasco and his fleet anchored before the city of Goa. The situation in the most important possession in Portuguese Asia had deteriorated into partisan infighting as a result, in part, of the corruption of the Menezes regime. One of D. Duarte's boon companions, Francisco Pereira Pestana, was captain of Goa, and his abuses had alienated many of the leading members of the Indo-Portuguese community there. In particular, he had an ongoing feud with many of the foremost *casado*s (married Portuguese settlers). These problems, and the absence of D. Duarte in Hurmuz, had resulted in the loss of surrounding areas of Ponda and Salsette to the troops of the king of Bijapur, Isma'il Adil Shah (r. 1510–34) in 1523. Pereira Pestana had offered little effective resistance to this attack and had merely sought a truce.

The arrival of D. Vasco was greeted with much enthusiasm by those in Goa who wanted to end the corruption of D. Duarte and his cohorts. The new Viceroy was received with much pomp and ceremony, which he clearly relished. "[T]he city gave him a great reception with festivities and a rich canopy, and a speech, and they bore him in procession to the cathedral; and they conveyed him with rejoicings to the fortress." The Captain, despite his other shortcomings, had evidently kept the fortress "in very good order." Pereira had sought to curry favor with D. Vasco by meeting him aboard ship at the bar of the Mandovi river and accompanying him upriver to the city. But his efforts were in vain. Upon entering the fortress, the Viceroy told him "Senhor Francisco Pereira, I should wish to find all your affairs kept thus in as good order as these buildings." On the next day, he replaced him as Captain with D. Henrique de Meneses.

During his stay in Goa, D. Vasco sought to impress the king's subjects with the wealth and power that could be won legitimately in the service of the Crown. Correia, who lived in India for many years in this period, provided great detail and insight on these matters. "The said Dom Vasco brought great state, being served by men bearing silver maces, by a major-domo, and two pages with chains of gold, many equerries and body servants, very well-dressed and cared for." This was certainly a far cry from the rather pathetic state of his arrival in Calicut in 1498. In true noble, or even royal, fashion, the Viceroy extended this lavish display to his table as well. "He had a rich table service of silver, and fine Flanders tapestry, and the cover of the table at which he dined was of brocade." The Viceroy traveled with a guard of two hundred men, with gilded pikes and dressed in his livery. This display was intended not only for the benefit of the king's subjects in the *Estado da India*, but also for the consumption of the indigenous rulers of India. The count had learned a valuable lesson as early as his first voyage: Such display mattered a great deal in winning diplomatic and financial largesse from Indian rulers. By 1524, he had the means to excel at this game, and excel he did.

D. João III had given D. Vasco plenary powers over judicial, executive, and administrative matters. The Viceroy's harsh reputation, well earned on his first two voyages, had no doubt preceded him. Upon his arrival in India, da Gama was already both respected and feared. As four members of the Goa Council wrote: "The Count of Vidigueira arrived at this city on the twenty-third day of September . . . It seems to us that he comes with good designs, and desirous to serve Your Highness and to do justice to suitors, which is very requisite for this country." The Viceroy acted swiftly and effectively to correct the abuses he found. As opposed to recent practice, what had most impressed the residents of Goa was the fact that D. Vasco had refused all forms of "gifts" offered to him. "Many persons went to him with offerings such as it is customary to make to governors when they are newly arrived; he would not take anything from Christian or Moor, and still less from this city, which we all looked upon as extraordinary."

Among other things, the Viceroy sought to correct the worrying abuse of the king's officers and captains, who sold royal artillery to private merchants to use on their own vessels. D. Vasco issued firm orders that all such weapons would have to be returned within thirty days under the penalty of losing both one's property and life. Most of these weapons were indeed returned. Many men had been using the royal hospital built near the gate of St. Catherine as a form of free lodging. These men were forced out, and the doctors ordered "not to take in any sick person unless he were afflicted with sores or wounds." Da Gama also issued instructions that anyone injured in a brawl could not be admitted "saying that they brawled on account of women, and for that reason were not to be cured in the hospital." Da Gama also took a firm stance to resolve a festering dispute between Francisco Pereira and more than a dozen members of the *casado* community in Goa regarding confiscated property and other exactions.

D. Vasco had come out from Lisbon with an impressive group of nobles to restaff key positions throughout the *Estado da India*. In addition to installing Christovão de Souza at Chaul and D. Henrique de Meneses at Goa, the new Viceroy appointed capable captains for Cochin, Melaka, and Cannanur. Both D. Duarte and his predecessor, D. Diogo Lopes de Sequeira, had sought to deplete the powers of the chief financial officer for the Crown in the *Estado*, the *vedor da fazenda*. This policy had facilitated their ill-gotten gains at the expense of the king. D. João III and D. Vasco were determined to restore the powers of this office, second only to that of Viceroy, and in doing so to crack down on fiscal abuses. The man chosen for this task was Afonso Meixa. Meixa had formidable credentials: He had been D. Manuel's factor at the fort of São Jorge da Mina. In the process, he had become rich, a knight of the Order of Christ, and a man with powerful connections at court. Meixa was well acquainted with D. Vasco and shared his views on reform. As Correia noted: "The Viceroy was very zealous for the King's revenue, and used to say that men came to India very poor and enriched themselves; and that he, if he could, would make the King rich, as the greatest benefit the people could obtain was to have their King well supplied." Da Gama also sought to apply stricter standards in granting offices in the growing bureaucracy of the *Estado*. "Before giving them their charges, he used to question and examine them, and if they did not give a good account of themselves, and show themselves for the discharge of their offices, he did not commit them to them." D. Vasco also forced men nominated for the office of clerk "to write in his presence, and if he was not a good writer he did not give it to him, and would say that if a man wrote badly and begged for a clerkship, it was only for the purpose of evildoing."

During his relatively brief stay in Goa, the Viceroy also sought to consolidate the military position of this valued possession, which was periodically threatened by the sultanate of Bijapur. He sailed from Lisbon with "large supplies for the magazines, and much artillery, and armories of white weapons, rich cuirasses and firelocks." These armaments bolstered Portuguese fortresses in India. To attract Portuguese soldiers who had deserted to return "to the service of God and the King," he offered a three-month amnesty. To encourage military service on the part of the Portuguese *casados*, he would only underwrite their pay and rations if "there was a war in which they fought, or . . . they went aboard the fleets." To instill greater discipline in the ranks, he "proclaimed that no seafaring man should wear a cloak except on a Sunday or Saint's Day on going to church, and if they did they should be put at the pump-break for a day in disgrace." D. Vasco also ordered that "every man who drew pay as a matchlock man should wear his match fastened to his arm." At the same time, he "upbraided the men-at-arms very much for wearing cloaks, because with them they did not look like soldiers."

In Goa, the Viceroy clearly reinforced the pretensions of the Crown toward controlling the Indian Ocean trade by confirming the king's monopoly over vital products and in enforcing the *cartaz* system. D. Vasco "proclaimed that, under the pain of death and loss of property, no one should navigate without his license." All shipowners were obliged to "make contracts and shipments with the King's factors, with the papers that should be requisite, and that without this they should not navigate; and that any man who traded with the property of an officer of the King, whether an officer of justice or of exchequer, should lose his ship and all his property to the King, and should be banished forever to Portugal." This was done, Correira explained, "because the King had need of the trade of India." The revenues and profits from this trade for the Crown would in turn provide the "wherewith to pay the services of the men in India, and to oblige them to serve in the fleets."

Perhaps the most controversial act that the Viceroy took in Goa was to punish the three women who had sailed from Lisbon and been turned over to him in Mozambique. Upon reaching Goa, D. Vasco ordered that these women be flogged in public with a city crier proclaiming: "The justice of the King our Sovereign! It orders these women to be flogged, because they had no fear of his justice, and crossed over to India in spite of his prohibition." When word of this punishment spread, there was something of an outcry in the city against this act, as European women were exceedingly rare in the enclave. "All the gentlemen, and the bishop, and the friars, and the brothers of mercy interceded on behalf of these women, and good men offered three thousand *pardaos* for the ransom of captives." On the day that the sentence was to be carried out, the "brothers of mercy and the Franciscan friars came with a crucifix to beg for the women to be given up to them." This act upset D. Vasco greatly and he berated the clerics, telling them "not to let such a thing happen to them again." Given the Viceroy's crusade to restore order in the *Estado da India*, it is not surprising that he rejected all such appeals. "So he commanded that the women should be flogged, saying, that he would punish with rigorous justice in this world, and that the Lord would have mercy in the next on whomsoever was deserving of it." As D. Vasco explained, "Never shall they meet with anything from me except severity and punishment." Although this public flogging of the women whipped on a yoke scandalized many in Goa, the Viceroy achieved his main objective: "but seeing such great firmness in carrying out his will, they felt great fear, and were wary, and reformed many evils which existed in India, especially among the gentlemen who were very dissolute and evil-doers."

From Goa to Cochin, October–December 1524

After undertaking these substantial reforms in Goa, the Viceroy departed aboard a new galliot that had just been built sometime around October 21, 1524. As he had done in Chaul, he left strict orders with his new Captain, D. Henrique, that if D. Duarte appeared he would not be allowed to land, nor should he follow any of Duarte's orders. On the voyage south along the west coast of India, the Viceroy's fleet came upon a fleet commanded by D. Luis de Menezes, the Governor's brother. D. Luis was sailing north to Goa to rendezvous with D. Duarte, who was expected soon from Hurmuz. Da Gama, however, forced this fleet to accompany him south toward Cochin. On the voyage, D. Vasco also used some smaller ships to reconnoiter the river's mouths at Mangalor and Barcelor. He left at least six ships with Jeronymo de Sousa and others under Manuel de Macedo to take "possession of the bars of these rivers." The fleet then called at Cannanur at the end of October. Here, the

Viceroy received a warm welcome "with pomp and honors" from the Kolattiri, who "was much pleased to see him." The Kolattiri was obviously impressed that the discoverer of India had returned and also no doubt relished the past defeats da Gama had inflicted on his rival, the Samudri of Calicut. At Cannanur, D. Simão de Meneses was installed as Captain. The Viceroy remained there for three days and, among other things, also threatened reprisals for any "raiding" activities against Portuguese ships. The fleet departed, and, after passing by Calicut at night, reached Cochin sometime in early November.

Upon reaching Cochin, the Viceroy was in a strong position to continue his reform program and to deal with the man who embodied the institutional abuses that had been weakening the empire: D. Duarte de Meneses. D. Vasco had the tremendous prestige that his accomplishments in India conferred upon him. He was now a count, wealthy, one of the noble elite. The young king had given him very wide powers as Viceroy and had ordered his reform campaign. Finally, da Gama's past reputation for ruthless behavior made men fear him and only added to his aura. In short, he appeared unassailable as he neared Cochin. Unfortunately, at this culminating moment of his life and career, D. Vasco's health began to fail him. Pêro Nunes, the long-suffering *vedor da fazenda*, "went out to sea in a large boat with an awning, and dressed out, to land the Viceroy." The two eventually met near Cranganor, and da Gama received "him with great honor" and in turn he gave the Viceroy "a long account of the affairs of the governor and of all India." The next day, D. Vasco was received with much pomp and ceremony in the roadstead of Cochin. According to Correa's account, D. Luis in particular made a great display, whether sincere or not, firing more than a hundred rounds from the guns of his galleon. The following day, the Viceroy made his formal entrance into the town. He went to the main church and was greeted by the leading Portuguese residents. Finally, he met the king of Cochin. The ruler, "on seeing him, dismounted from the elephant on which he came, and embraced the Viceroy several times." D. Vasco then established his residence in the fortress and "occupied himself with the dispatch of business."

Among the first orders of business in Cochin was to replace the Captain, D. Garcia de Noronha, a nephew of Afonso de

Albuquerque, with D. Lope Vaz de Sampaio. The powerful Afonso Meixa replaced Péro Nunes as *vedor da fazenda* in December 1524. In the accounts of Correia and Castanheda, the Viceroy and D. João III were both happy with the conduct of Nunes, at least with his skills in procuring good-quality pepper for shipment to Lisbon. During his six years in office, "he had sent pepper of such quality that in the kingdom it suffered a loss of 7 or 8%, whilst at first it lost 30 or 40%." The Mappila merchants, who had initially acted as middlemen in the pepper trade for the Portuguese, had sought to increase their profits by selling the Europeans pepper that was "damp, green" and mixed with "sand and grit." According to most accounts, Nunes had begun the practice of buying the pepper from St. Thomas Christians along the coast with direct contacts with the producers, thus leading to a notable decrease in the amount of waste in the cargoes that went to Portugal. Predictably, the Mappila merchants had not been amused by this sound business decision. D. Vasco did everything he could to cultivate the ties with these Syrian Christians.

It seems likely that in addition to correcting the worrying abuses in the *Estado da India*, D. Vasco also traveled to India with orders to conduct a definitive campaign of aggression against the Samudri of Calicut and his allies on the coast of Kerala. As Correia wrote: "The Viceroy entertained serious thoughts of carrying on a great war in all the coasts and rivers of the Indian shores as soon as he should have finished dispatching the ships to the kingdom." Some successes were achieved during late 1524. The captain of the Portuguese fort in Calicut, D. João de Lima, was badly in need of assistance. D. Vasco sent out a fleet of galleys under Jeronimo de Sousa, and his force defeated a Mappila fleet under the command of Kutti Ali of Kappatt. Meanwhile, D. Jorge Telo, commanding a fleet patrolling near Goa, procured a good quality of pepper in captured ships heading from Calicut to Gujarat. Indeed, he was able to dispatch much of this pepper to Afonso Meixa in Cochin to assist loading the ships returning to Lisbon in early 1525.

That da Gama was in a bellicose mindset was clear to all those in Cochin. "The Viceroy showed himself very well disposed to warlike men, and used to say that when he went to fight, he would not give the captaincies except to men who in war had shown themselves as good soldiers." His deteriorating health, however, prevented him from leading the large expedition he wanted against the Samudri. This task would only be undertaken, and with a good deal of success, under D. Henriques de Meneses in 1525.

Meanwhile, in December 1524, D. Duarte had at long last appeared before Cochin. The Governor's return trip from Hurmuz had been leisurely, with stops in Maskat, Diu, Chaul, Goa, and Bhatkal. D. Vasco's appointees as Governors in Chaul and Goa, Cristovão de Sousa and D. Henrique de Meneses, had followed their instructions well and both received D. Duarte in an exceedingly cold fashion. For his part, the Governor no doubt knew that trouble awaited him in Cochin. Perhaps because he had heard of the Viceroy's fragile health, he was in no hurry to complete his journey south. At the same time, his brother, D. Luis de Meneses, had utilized his time in Cochin in a vain attempt to lobby D. Vasco. Even though D. Luis would be forced to relinquish the title of Captain-major of the Indian Seas to the young and inexperienced D. Estêvão da Gama, he diligently played the diplomat in late 1524. In his frequent visits to the Viceroy, he always touched "upon the affairs of his brother, in order to see if he could moderate matters so that the Viceroy should not conduct himself very rigorously with his brother." Da Gama, however, was clearly not swayed by these entreaties and "always spoke to him of the excellencies of strict justice and showed his intention of observing it rigidly." The Viceroy "had full powers to execute justice for all crimes, upon all persons who were within the Cape of Good Hope, without sending them to Portugal to be judged by the King, for he would execute justice upon the King's own brothers, if he had them in India." This was obviously not the response that D. Luis was hoping to hear and for which he had expended such vast quantities of shot and powder.

By the time of D. Duarte's arrival, the Viceroy's health had deteriorated. Nevertheless, he took a hard line with the Governor and even initially forbade him from landing. A committee led by Afonso Meixa and Lopo Vaz de Sampaio went aboard his ship and presented the Governor with several letters; one was from D. João, dated Feburary 1524 and written in Évora; the other was from D. Vasco. The king's rather rambling letter ordered D. Duarte to return immediately to Portugal and to hand over all power and authority to da Gama as soon as he reached India. Upon doing so, he should provide a formal list of all of the ships, artillery, munitions, and soldiers to da Gama. It then outlined various scenarios regarding D. Duarte's movements if he should miss the sailing of the return fleet to Lisbon. D. Vasco's letter was much more strident, among other things, instructing him not to leave his ship and specifying that he should return to Lisbon aboard the ship *Castello*. Correia, who was probably present in Cochin for these events, put the situation in more stark terms. Menezes "had to go to the kingdom a prisoner upon his parole that he would not go out of it [the *Castello*] except in Lisbon, upon a message from the King, and that he was to go and put himself on board the ship, and in it give this pledge signed by himself."

D. Duarte, a haughty noble from a well-established family, did not take kindly to the tone or contents of da Gama's letter. He berated several members of the delegation, whom he viewed as social inferiors. With a good deal of relish, he also reminded Lopo Vaz de Sampaio that it had been his father, D. João de Menezes, a count-prior, who had made him cavalier in North Africa on the field of battle. "You ought to remember that my father made you a knight, and that you cannot therefore be against his affairs." For a time, Menezes flatly refused to move his baggage and goods from the ship, *São Jorge*, which he had decided was the most suitable for his return voyage. Upon hearing this, D. Vasco declared: "D. Duarte has bad advice in the course he is following with me, and is placing himself in a position in which his misfortunes may become greater . . . since he wishes to follow out his fancy, he will hear of me." The Viceroy then had the chief constable and auditor-general prepare two galleons with artillery. These ships anchored on either side of the *São Jorge*, and the chief constable was to require D. Duarte "on the part of the King to come out at once and go and place himself on board the ship *Castello*." If he did not obey after three warnings, the chief constable and auditor-general would "return to the galleons, and with the artillery send the ship to the bottom."

At this point, D. Luis evidently sought to intercede on behalf of his brother with the Viceroy. He "entreated him not to conduct himself so rigorously with his brother, since he had not sold any of the King's fortresses; and the things ordered with such wrath, rather resembled hatred than any other good reason." But D. Vasco, true to his character to the end, would not desist: "Senhor

Dom Luis, if your brother had sold fortresses, he would not have his head where it is now, for I would have ordered it to be cut off." The Viceroy also berated the younger Menezes for uttering "that speech to me; neither did your brother ever annoy me, for me to feel hatred towards him." In D. Vasco's view the only mistake he could commit "so God give me health" was in "not doing all that I am obliged to do." As he declared, "I act thus because I am your servant, and the King our sovereign is your friend." In the future, D. Duarte should pay greater obedience "to the commands of the King, since up to this time he has observed them so ill in the governance of India that he is the scandal of Portugal." If D. Duarte obeyed his commands, all would go well. At that point, D. Vasco wished to end the conversation, but D. Luis persisted and finally stormed out, declaring: "You do not choose to hear me. I trust in God that a time will come in which I also shall not choose to hear you. I will go to my brother, and whatever happens to him shall happen to me." In response to this affront, D. Vasco had Lopo Vaz de Sampaio conduct D. Luis, alone, to the beach in order to be embarked with his brother. Once aboard the *São Jorge*, he convinced his older brother to transfer himself and his possession to the *Castello*.

By December 4, 1524, Menezes finally and formally recognized the transfer of power that had taken place upon the Viceroy's arrival at Chaul several months earlier. It is clear that both D. Duarte and D. Luis harbored great hopes that the Viceroy would soon expire and that their name would appear in the letters of succession D. Vasco carried with him. Other nobles in Cochin at the time had similar hopes, including Lopo Vaz de Sampaio and Pêro Mascarenhas, the new captain for Melaka, who had not yet left from India for his post. For the remainder of December, the Viceroy did his best to continue with his duties, but his worsening condition meant that a group of his supporters, led by Afonso Meixa, helped prepare the return fleet for Lisbon and other fleets destined to enforce the *cartaz* monopoly that the Crown and the Viceroy were so keen to uphold. As in Goa, D. Vasco discovered that there was not sufficient artillery to outfit the coastal fleets so he issued a decree ordering, "under the pain of death" that all royal artillery be returned and by "this means a large quantity of artillery was collected." In early December, the Viceroy sent a ship back to Lisbon with dispatches and a cargo of spices under Francisco de Mendonça. He also spent time in December seeking to obtain some of the treasure that D. Duarte had carried back with him from his Hurmuz enterprise. According to a letter of January 1, 1525, by Vicente Pegado, the secretary of the *Estado da India*, this treasure was supposedly comprised of 100,000 *pardaos* in tribute, 30,000 *pardaos* from a prize ship in the Persian Gulf, and another 15,000 *cruzados* originally sent from Lisbon to purchase spices. The wily D. Duarte not only managed to withhold this booty from D. Vasco; he also prevented D. João III from obtaining it after his return to Portugal.

Illness and Death of Vasco da Gama

Sensing that death was near, D. Vasco moved his residence from the fortress to the house of Diogo Pereira, located near the church courtyard. The Viceroy recognized that he did not have long to live and therefore took measures to ensure a smooth transition of power. In particular, he wanted to prevent D. Duarte from regaining power if there was a lapse in authority. After all, one of the main objectives of his viceregal appointment was to restore order and a more efficient administrative system for the empire, and this he was determined to do. To that end, according to Barros, he had a deed prepared, sworn to, and signed by Afonso Meixa and others that stated that in case of his death, Lopo Vaz de Sampaio would serve as Governor until the person named in the royal letters of succession should reach India to assume power. If that person were already in India, his son, D. Estevão, would present him "with a box of papers belonging to the King." In Correia's account, D. Vasco prepared detailed minutes giving "all the regulations for what they [Meixa and Sampaio] had to do until they gave way to the governor who might succeed." Once these official preparations were made, D. Vasco could attend to the more personal arrangements occasioned by the approach of death.

The Viceroy "confessed and took the holy sacrament with much perfection as a Catholic Christian." He also spent time on his last testament. Before his departure, D. Vasco had wisely seen to the rapid assumption of his eldest son, D. Francisco, to his titles and estates in Portugal upon his death. In his testament in Cochin, he ordered D. Estêvão and D. Paulo to return to the kingdom aboard the fleet of January 1525. They were "to take away all his goods, and sell nothing, and to take away all his servants; and those who wished to remain, they were to pay them all their pay from the King for the services which they had rendered." All of his clothes and household furniture of silk were to be given to the churches and hospitals. Of particular note was the fact that, according to Correia, he bequeathed 100,000 *reais* each to the women he had had flogged in Goa, "which were to be given them with much secrecy." If these women rejected the money, it was to be "doubled and given to the house of Holy Mercy." These women used D. Vasco's money as dowries; they "found good husbands, and were married, and became honest women." Overall, he set his affairs in order "like a good Christian, with all the sacraments of the Church." The Viceroy ordered that his bones "should be conveyed to the kingdom." With "full understanding" he finally "delivered up his soul on the night of Christmas of the holy birth of Christ, at three o'clock after midnight on the twenty-fourth day of December of this present year of 1524. God be praised."

Epilogue

Vasco da Gama's death on Christmas Eve of 1524 was kept secret "without weeping and lamentations" while suitable preparations were made. Then his sons made the announcement, and most of the Portuguese in Cochin came to the church square "and each one showed what he felt." D. Vasco's body was dressed in a manner befitting and reflecting the great social and financial strides he had made in his lifetime. "The body [was] dressed in silk clothes, and over them a mantle of the Order of Christ, with a sword and gilded belt, and gilt spurs fixed upon dark buskins, and on its head a dark round barret-cap." His sons and other nobles "clothed in the mantles of their orders," carried the body, followed by the crowd, to the Franciscan church of Santo Antonio (St. Anthony), where the Viceroy was buried in the main chapel. The next day, a great service was held in which "all the gentlemen were present, and his sons were placed amongst the friars, and at night they betook themselves to the monastery and made their lamentations as was reasonable on losing so honored a father, and of such great desert in the kingdom of Portugal."

D. Estêvão da Gama and D. Paulo da Gama, following their father's wishes, sailed with the annual pepper fleet from Cochin in late January 1525. D. Duarte de Meneses and D. Luis de Meneses also departed for Lisbon aboard these ships. Their hopes for regaining power had been dashed once the royal letters of succession had been opened. Soon after D. Vasco's funeral, the leading nobles gathered at the cathedral in Cochin, and Afonso Meixa provided the sealed letter from the king dated February 10, 1524. Since da Gama was the first Viceroy or Governor to die in office before a successor had been named, this ceremony marked the first time that this system was utilized in the government of the *Estado da In-*

dia. The letter of succession named the recently installed Captain of Goa, D. Henrique de Meneses, as the new Governor. D. Henrique left Francisco de Sá as Captain of Goa and headed south to Cochin, but he did not arrive before the departure of the fleet of 1525. Nevertheless, for the next few months, D. Henrique fulfilled D. Vasco's pledge to attack and reduce the power of Calicut and the Mappila settlements along the coast. Commanding a force of more than 1500 Portuguese troops, he brutally and successfully diminished the power of the Samudri and his allies. D. Vasco would no doubt have approved. The main objectives of his final voyage, a voyage for which he had risked much, had been achieved.

The attempt to gauge the impact of any single individual on great historical events is always difficult. Vasco da Gama's life and career pose this problem for historians. Perhaps the best way to judge da Gama's impact on world history is to compare the Portugal of his youth with that at the time of his death. In the 1470s, the kingdom was a marginal European power with few natural resources, a small population, and limited sources of wealth. By 1524, Portugal had been transformed into a leading European power with a lucrative *global* empire that stretched from Brazil, along the African coast, through the Persian Gulf region, to India, Indonesia, and China. In this revolutionary process, networks and methods had been established for the transfer of trading products, ideas, disease pools, flora and fauna, military technology, and religion.

Vasco da Gama played a crucial role in that startling transformation. He deserves substantial credit for taking perhaps the most difficult step in that process. It was *his* epic 1497 voyage that inaugurated the presence of the Europeans in Indian Ocean affairs and trade. Thereafter, his 1502 voyage clearly demonstrated the dominance of European firepower in Asian waters, a technological reality that quickly resulted in the conquest of this vast empire. Finally, his 1524 voyage fulfilled the need for reform in an increasingly unwieldy empire, which helped it survive into the seventeenth century and beyond. At the same time, Vasco da Gama's family and fortune rose along with those of Portugal. Starting from humble provincial beginnings, his daring, skills, and ruthlessness won him and his family a title, vast estates, and great renown. These exploits and services to the Crown secured his family's social and economic position for the next five centuries in Portugal. Da Gama therefore lived a notable and successful life. Moreover, he played an important role in the process of creating the global economy and society in which we live today.

By virtue of his many accomplishments, Vasco da Gama quickly passed into the realm of legend for the Portuguese people. This process began almost immediately after his death. Correia, writing soon afterward, declared: "For it pleased the Lord to give this man so strong a spirit, that without any human fear he passed through so many perils of death during the discovery of India, as is related in his history; all for the love of the Lord, for the great increase of his Catholic faith, and for the great honor and glory of ennobling Portugal." By the 1560s, old Portuguese *fidalgos* like D. Jorge de Castro, who had sailed with D. Vasco on his final voyage, were writing nostalgically on the prosperity of places like Cochin "when Dom Vasco da Guama came to these parts as viceroy." By the 1580s, Luíz Vaz de Camões completed the process of elevating da Gama into the pantheon of Portuguese heroes by making the 1497–1499 voyage the focal point of his great lyrical poem *The Lusiads*. D. Vasco survived on that lofty pedestal as long as the Portuguese empire in Asia survived. In fact, it was only after the fall of Goa to India in 1961 and during the period of decolonization of Portuguese Africa in the 1970s that this position came under attack. Although some revisionist historians have sought to modify his stature as one of the great figures of the late medieval and early modern period, D. Vasco has largely and deservedly survived this campaign unscathed. Today in Portugal, he retains a good deal of the aura that Camões helped to bestow upon him nearly half a millennium ago.

Strangely, while D. Vasco's legend was secure within a generation of his death, his physical remains underwent a far more circuitous journey to the pantheon of Portuguese heroes: the Monastery of Belém. In his last testament, the Viceroy declared that his bones should be sent home. In fact, they remained at the church of Santo Antonio in Cochin until 1539, when they were returned to Portugal. The Viceroy had made arrangements prior to his 1524 voyage for his remains to be buried in the old Church of Our Lady of the Relics in Vidigueira. In 1533, D. Francisco da Gama, his son and second count of Vidigueira, had funded in perpetuity a daily mass at the church for the souls of his parents. In 1593, a new church of Our Lady of the Relics was finished, and D. Vasco's remains were again moved. D. Miguel da Gama, the

Viceroy's grandson, oversaw this transfer to the ossuary on the epistle (or right side as one faces the altar) side of the chancel. A stone lid was placed above with the epitaph: "*Aqui Jaz o Grande Argonavta Dom Vasco da Gama Pr. Conde da Vidigvera Almirante das Indias Orientaes e Seu Famoso Descobridor.*" This epitaph translates as "Here Lies the Great Argonaut Dom Vasco da Gama, First Count of Vidigueira Admiral of the East Indies and its Famous Discoverer."

The bones of D. Vasco remained in the new church of Our Lady of the Relics in Vidigueira for more than 280 years. In May 1834, the church was included in a decree suppressing the number of Portuguese religious institutions and fell into decay. Grave robbers stole what they deemed of value and scattered the bones in the graves. In 1841, a new owner purchased the property and restored the church. Soon after, a campaign began to transfer D. Vasco's remains to a more fitting resting place, the Monastery of Jeronimos at Belém. In the 1870s, the historian A.C. Teixeira de Aragão championed this cause. In 1880, to commemorate the tercentenary of the death of the poet Camões, da Gama's remains, along with those of that great national literary figure, were buried at Belém.

However, the transfer of da Gama's remains was hardly scientific. As soon as the seals to the grave were broken, it was obvious that the bones, due to the ravages of earlier desecrators, were a confused mess. As Teixeira de Aragão wrote: "We had hardly time to place the bones in the casket, but observed that there were skulls, thighbones and leg bones which appeared to belong to four skeletons." Nevertheless, these bones were put in a sandalwood casket, and with much ceremony the procession began toward Belém. There, on June 8, 1880, king D. Luis conducted both caskets to their new resting places. A silver wreath was placed on D. Vasco's casket, and it was assumed that at last he had found a suitable resting place with the heroes of Portugal.

But this was not the end of the story. Although the royal commission had opened the grave on the epistle side of the chancel and the stone lid had the name of the Viceroy on it, Teixeira de Aragão's curiosity had been aroused. Soon after, he found a seventeenth-century manuscript belonging to the Monastery of Our Lady of the Relics. In it, he found the following lines: "The first lord of the House of Vidigueira, whom we have to place among those who are buried in this monastery of Our Lady of the Relics, is the great Dom Vasco da Gama, founder of the house of the Counts of Vidigueira . . . This monastery has care for these bones in the chance, on the evangelist (left facing the altar) side near the great altar . . . He has no inscription on his grave." Moreover, the manuscript stated that Vasco da Gama rested "in a grave lined with black velvet and covered with a pall of black velvet." Teixeira de Aragão also found an eighteenth-century source that stated that D. Vasco's grave was on the evangelist side. So, in July 1884, he returned to the church and raised the tombstone on the evangel side and found "fragments of a chest lined with black trimmed velvet, and with gilded nails, the existence of the bones belonged to a single skeleton." Although Teixeira de Aragão was convinced that he had found the true remains of D. Vasco, it took until 1898, the fourth centenary of the discovery of the sea route of India, for the government to correct this mistake. In May of that year, D. Vasco's bones were finally and correctly placed in a marble sepulcher decorated with the arms of the da Gama family in the Jeronomite Monastery at Belém. The Viceroy was depicted according to Correia's description of his original funeral in Cochin in 1524. Appropriately, the inscription was from the *Lusíadas*: "*Partimos nos assi do sancto templo/Que nas praias do mar está assentado/Que o nome tem da terra, para exemplo/Donde Deus foi em carne ao mundo dado.*" "Thus we departed from the Holy Fane/That on the margins of the sea rests/Which land, by way of example, has the name/where God came to this world in the flesh."

Da Gama's Tomb, Church of Monastery of Jeronimos, Belem. (Glenn J. Ames)

A Note on the Sources

In an attempt to make the events in this book, which took place nearly half a millennium ago, more vivid for the contemporary reader, I have included a large number of quotations from both manuscript sources and the main sixteenth-century chronicler accounts. Because there are so few surviving documents produced by Vasco da Gama himself, some of the main sources for his life since the mid-sixteenth century have been the Portuguese chronicler accounts of that period. The direct quotations in this book have been taken from those accounts, along with others from the *Roteiro* of da Gama's first voyage to India. Of the chronicler accounts, one of the best is that of João de Barros (1496–1570), called *Decades of Asia*. Barros had been educated at court by leading Portuguese humanists, and in his early twenties had written a chivalric romance with the assistance of Prince João (later D. João III). He traveled to the Portuguese African outpost at Mina and, in 1532, Barros received the important bureaucratic post of factor of the India House in Lisbon. By all accounts, he was a fair and able administrator. As a reward, Barros had been given an important imperial appointment in Brazil. But a large armada that he had helped outfit was lost in 1539, and this disaster devastated him financially. As a result, he accepted a royal offer to write an official history of the Portuguese in Asia for D. João III. The first *Decade* of his *Ásia* appeared in 1552; the second in 1553; the third in 1563; and the fourth, of more dubious authorship, only in 1615.

153

Although Barros never traveled to Asia, his connections at court as well as his years at the India House afforded him access to many manuscript documents in compiling his history. His *Decades* were continued by Diogo do Couto (1542–1616). Couto was born in Lisbon and studied at the Jesuit College of Santo Antão during the reign of D. João II. Unlike Barros, Couto sailed for India in 1559 and again in 1571. He had settled down and married in the Portuguese Asian capital of Goa. In 1595, Couto became royal chronicler and chief archivist of the rich archives (*Torre do Tombo da Índia*) there. Based on his research in India, he added five volumes to Barros's *Decades* before his death in 1616. Three more volumes were published between 1736 and 1778. Couto's *Decades* covered the period 1526–1600, and his historical approach was much more critical in nature than that of Barros.

Damião de Góis (1502–1574) was another leading Portuguese humanist of this period who chronicled the career of Vasco da Gama. Góis served João III in a variety of diplomatic posts throughout Europe beginning in 1523. These travels allowed him to meet many of the leading intellectual figures of the northern Renaissance and Reformation, including Martin Luther and Erasmus. Albrecht Dürer painted his portrait. After taking a degree from the University of Padua in 1532, Góis spent the next decade living in Flanders. During this period, he published *Commentarius Rerum gestarum in India citra Gangem a Lusitanis* (1539). Captured by the French during the siege of Louvain in 1542, he obtained his freedom thanks to a heavy ransom and, as a reward for his services, was granted a coat of arms by the Habsburg emperor Charles V. Góis returned to Portugal in 1545, and three years later he was appointed chief keeper of the royal archives and chronicler to the king. In 1558, he began a history of the reign of Manuel I, *Chronica do felicissimo Rey Dom Manoel*, which was published in four parts in 1567 and 1568. Like Barros and Couto, Góis had extensive access to the relevant documentation in compiling his work. His historical objectivity, which alienated some powerful interests in Portugal, and past associations in northern Europe resulted in his arrest by the Inquisition in 1571. After serving a sentence of forced seclusion at the monastery of Batalha, he was released but died suddenly in January 1574.

Of all the chroniclers who describe Vasco da Gama's life, only Gaspar Correia (1495–1561?) had the benefit of actually witnessing part of da Gama's career in Asia. Correia traveled to India in ca. 1513 and served as secretary to Afonso do Albuquerque during his governorship (1509–1515). Correia compiled his *Lendas da India* between ca. 1540 and his death in Goa sometime in the early 1560s. Correia based his history of Portuguese Asia on manuscript sources as well as diaries and personal papers he examined in Goa. Perhaps the most important of these documents was the diary of the priest João Figueira, who accompanied Vasco da Gama on his first voyage. Correia personally witnessed many of the key events in India during da Gama's third voyage of 1524. Since he intended to have the manuscript published posthumously, Correia's account offers a fairly objective analysis of the establishment of Portuguese power in India and da Gama's career. His dating of events, however, sometimes differs from the other chroniclers. Fernão Lopes da Castanheda (1500?–1559) only traveled to India in 1528 after da Gama's death. His *Historia do descobrimento e conquista da India pelos Portugueses* (1551–61) was nevertheless based on extensive research with manuscript documents in India and discussions with eyewitnesses. Castanheda's history covered the period from 1497 until 1549, and he was very meticulous in his dating of events. Since his account was published before all the others, it enjoyed a wide audience and perhaps influenced the works of Barros and Gois. Finally, Jerónimo Osório (1506–1580) was a leading literary figure and Latinist who was named bishop of Silves in 1564. Three years later, Osório was asked to adapt the work of Damião de Gois in Latin so that the deeds of the Portuguese in Asia might have a wider audience. In 1571, his *De rebus, Emmanuelis Regis* was published in Lisbon.

When these chronicler accounts are utilized carefully by the historian, they can be of fundamental importance for detailing and analyzing the life and career of Vasco da Gama. The quotations drawn from them can also hopefully help bring the period to life for the contemporary reader. In the suggested readings below, I have included existing English translations of the works of Barros, Couto, Goís, Correia, and Castanheda for those readers who might like to consult their accounts in detail but who do not read Portuguese.

Overall, the available literature on the history of Renaissance Portugal and the age of discoveries is vast. In English, good general surveys on Portuguese history include: H.V. Livermore, *A New History of Portugal* (Cambridge, 1976); A.H. Oliveira Marques, *History of Portugal* (2 vols., New York, 1972); and David Birmingham, *A Concise History of Portugal* (Cambridge, 1993). Some general works on the age of discovery and Portuguese expansion from ca. 1415–1550 include: F.C. Danvers, *The Portuguese in India* (2 vols., London, 1894); R.S. Whiteway, *The Rise of Portuguese Power in India, 1497–1550* (London, 1899, 1967); C.R. Boxer, *The Portuguese Seaborne Empire, 1415–1825* (New York, 1969); J.H. Parry, *The Age of Reconnaissance: Discovery, Exploration and Settlement 1450 to 1650* (London, 1963, 1981); *The European Reconnaissance: Selected Documents* (New York, 1968); G.D. Winius and B.W. Diffie, *Foundations of Portuguese Empire, 1415–1825* (Minneapolis, 1977); Sanjay Subrahmanyam, *The Portuguese Empire in Asia, 1500–1700* (Cambridge, 1990); M.N. Pearson, *The Portuguese in India* (Cambridge, 1987); and A.J.R. Russell-Wood, *The Portuguese Empire, 1415–1808* (Manchester and Baltimore, 1992, 1998). See also Peter Russell, *Prince Henry "The Navigator," A Life* (New Haven, 2000).

The Hakluyt Society in London has translated a number of the relevant contemporary accounts into English with exhaustive notes. Perhaps most importantly, see E.G. Ravenstein's *The Journal of the First Voyage of Vasco da Gama, 1497–1499* (London, 1898). Ravenstein's appendices provide much valuable information on the fleet. For example, Appendix D, pp. 157–70, details the ships of the fleet; Appendix E, pp. 173–81 provides a fascinating "Muster-roll" of the men aboard the ships; and Appendix G contains "Early Maps Illustrating Vasco da Gama's First Voyage." See also William Brooks Greenlee, *The Voyage of Pedro Ávares Cabral* (London, 1951); Gomes Eannes de Zurara, translated and edited by C.R. Beazley and Edgar Prestage, *The Chronicle of the Discovery and Conquest* of Guinea (2 vols., London, 1896); ed., and trans. by G.R. Crone, *The Voyages of Cadamosto* (London, 1937); and Duarte Pacheco Pereira, *Esmeraldo de situ orbis*, translated and edited by George H.T. Kimble (London, 1937). Finally, see also, Samuel Eliot Morison, "Sailing instructions of Vasco da Gama to Pedro Álvares Cabral," *The Mariner's Mirror* 24, 4 (1938), pp. 402–07.

English-language biographies of Vasco da Gama include Elaine Sanceau, *Good Hope: The Voyage of Vasco da Gama* (London, 1967); Henry H. Hart, *Sea Road to the Indies: An Account of the Voyages and Exploits of the Portuguese Navigators, Together with the Life and Times of Dom Vasco da Gama Capitao-Mor, Viceroy of India and Count of Vidigueira* (New York, 1950), and Sanjay Subrahmanyam, *The Career and Legend of Vasco da Gama* (Cambridge, 1997). For a concise summary of da Gama's life, see Francis A. Dutra, "A New Look at the Life and Career of Vasco da Gama," *Portuguese Studies Review*, Volume 6, No. 2 (Fall–Winter 1997–98), pp. 23–28. See also Anthony Disney, "Vasco da Gama's Reputation for Violence: The Alleged Atrocities at Calicut in 1502," *Indica* 32, 2 (1995), pp. 11–28.

For those who read Portuguese, see A.C. Teixeira de Aragão's classic ninteenth-century biography *Vasco da Gama e a Vidigueira* (Lisbon, 1871, 1886, 1898) and Luis Adão da Fonseca's more recent *Vasco da Gama: O Homem, A Viagem, a Epoca* (Lisbon, 1997). For the sixteenth-century chroniclers discussed above, see João de Barros, *Ásia. Décadas I–III* (3 volumes, Lisbon, 1945–46); Diogo do Couto, *Da Ásia. Décadas IV–XII* (facsimile of 1788 edition, Lisbon, 1974); Fernão Lopes da Castenheda, *História do descobrimento e conquista da Índia* (3 volumes, Coimbra, 1924–29), translated into English by Nicholas Lichefield as *The first Booke of the Historie of the Discoverie and Conquest of the East Indias* (London, 1582); Gaspar Correia, *Lendas da India* (4 volumes, Porto, 1975), translated into English by E.J. Stanley as *The Three Voyages of Vasco da Gama and His Viceroyalty* (New York, 1869); Damião de Góis, *Crónica do felicíssimo Rei D. Manuel* (Coimbra, 1949); and D. Jeronimo Osório, *Vida e feitos de El-Rei D. Manuel* (2 vols., Porto, 1944).

Major Personalities

Adil Shah, Yusuf: (r. 1489–1510) Sultan of the Muslim state of Bijapur. He launched a spirited counterattack to reclaim Goa in the spring of 1510.

D. Afonso V: King of Portugal (r. 1438–1481), nicknamed "the African" for his campaigns there against the Moors. Beginning in 1469, he leased further exploration of the west African coast to Fernão Gomes.

Albuquerque, Afonso de: (1453–1515) Principal creator of the *Estado da India* with his conquest of Hurmuz (1507/1515), Goa (1510), and Melaka (1511) during a brilliant career in Asia.

Almeida, D. Francisco de: (1450?–1510) First Viceroy of the *Estado* who sailed for India in 1505. Almeida reduced Kilwa and initiated trade with Melaka and Ceylon. He defeated a large Muslim fleet in 1509.

Almeida, D. Lourenco de: Son of D. Francisco de Almeida. Accompanied his father to India in 1505. He negotiated a trade agreement with Melaka and explored the island of Ceylon. In March 1508, D. Lourenco was killed in a battle with a Muslim fleet.

Ataíde, Dona Catarina de: Wife of Vasco da Gama, first countess of Vidigueira. Dona Catarina was the daughter of Álvaro de Ataíde, *alcaide* of Alvor, and Dona Maria da Silva. Their marriage produced seven children.

Cabral, Pedro Álvares: Commander of the (1467?–1519) second India fleet of 1500–01. On this voyage, Brazil was discovered and friendly relations established with Cochin and Cannanur.

Camões, Luis Vaz de: (1524?–1580) Portugal's greatest literary figure; served in North Africa (1547–49) before sailing for the *Estado da India* in 1553. Camões lived in Goa and Macau. He wrote the great epic poem, *Os Lusíadas* (1572), based on da Gama's first voyage.

Coelho, Nicolau: Commander of the ship *Berrio* in the 1497 fleet. He returned first to Lisbon in July 1499. Coelho sailed again to India in 1500 and 1503.

Cunha, Tristão da: (1460–1514?) Explorer and navigator who sailed to India in 1506. He established a fort on the island of Socotra to affect shipping in the Red Sea.

Da Gama, Estevão: Father of Vasco da Gama, *alcaide-mor* of Sines, knight of the Order of Santiago, and commander of Cercal. He was married to D. Isabel Sodré.

Da Gama, D. Estevão: Son of Vasco da Gama who accompanied his father on his 1524 return to India, with the title Captain-major of the Indian Seas.

Da Gama, Paulo: Brother of Vasco da Gama, commander of the ship *São Rafael* in the 1497 fleet. After greatly assisting his brother, he died in the Azores on the return voyage in 1499.

Dias, Bartolomeu: Explorer and navigator who made several voyages along the west African coast in the 1480s. He commanded the first European fleet to double the Cape of Good Hope (1487–1488). In 1500, he accompanied Cabral's fleet but died in a storm in the south Atlantic.

Emir Hussain: Kurdish admiral who command a large Muslim fleet on behalf of the Mamluks of Egypt in 1507–1509.

The fleet engaged the Portuguese first off Chaul (March 1508) and then off Diu (February 1509).

D. Fernando: Powerful younger brother of Afonso V, duke of Viseu, Grand Master of the Order of Santiago. He was the father of both D. Leonor, wife of D. João II, and king D. Manuel.

Henry, Prince: (1394–1460) Known as "the Navigator," third son of D. João I and Philippa of Lancaster, who accompanied his father in the conquest of Ceuta (1415). As Governor of the Algarve (1419) and Grand Master of the Order of Christ (1420), he funded a series of voyages along the west coast of Africa.

D. João I: First king in the Aviz dynasty (r. 1385–1433) in Portugal. D. João continued the reconquest against Islam by conquering the town of Ceuta in North Africa in 1415.

D. João II: King of Portugal (r. 1481–1495) who broke the power of the great nobles and supported the voyages of discovery down the African coast. He built the fort at S. Jorge da Mina on the Guinea coast.

D. João III: King of Portugal (r. 1521–1557), son of D. João II, who sought to correct abuses in the *Estado da India* by naming Vasco da Gama as Viceroy of India in 1524.

D. Jorge: Bastard son of D. João II. D. Jorge was Grand Master of the Order of Santiago and Aviz (1492) and duke of Coimbra (1500).

Magalhaes, Ferdinand: (or Magellan, 1480?–1521). Sailed for India in 1505 and took part in the capture of Goa and Melaka. After a dispute with D. Manuel, he offered his services to Charles V. In 1519, Magalhaes began his circumnavigation of the globe, which ended with his death in the Philippines in 1521.

D. Manuel I: King of Portugal (r. 1495–1521). Son of D. Fernando, duke of Viseu. Manuel was duke of Beja and Grand Master of the Order of Christ when be ascended the throne upon the death of his brother-in-law, D. João II.

Menezes, D. Duarte de: Governor of India (1522–1524) who supposedly found the tomb of the Apostle St. Thomas near

Madras. His corrupt practices attracted the attention of the Crown.

Menezes, D. Luis de: Brother of D. Duarte de Menezes. D. Luis sailed to India with his brother in 1521 and did much to harass Muslim shipping along the Indian coasts as Captain-major of the Indian Seas.

Nova, João de: Commander of the third India fleet, 1501–1502, which explored the coast of Brazil and east Africa before reaching the Malabar coast. He defeated a fleet of the Zamorin of Calicut (January 1502).

Sodré, Vincente: Uncle of Vasco da Gama, who commanded a five-ship squadron in the fourth India fleet of 1502–1503 with orders to harass Muslim shipping in the Arabian sea.

Timoja: (or Timmayya) Hindu corsair based at Honawar who harassed da Gama's fleet at the Anjedive islands in 1498 and then convinced Afonso de Albuquerque to attack Goa in 1510.

Glossary

Alcaide, Alcaide-mor: Governor or (higher-ranking) Governor-Major of a town or province with civil and military jurisdiction; from the Arabic *Al Kadi*, or Judge.

Alvará: Decree, usually issued by the Crown in the form of Letters Patent, certifying, authorizing, or confirming a particular act or request.

Bahar: Unit of weight measurement=approximately 459 lbs.

Bale: From the Arabic, *wali*, or Governor. In Calicut, the Zamorin's principal civil and police agent.

Camareiro-mor: Chief Chamberlain in the Military Orders of Christ, Avis, and Santiago with jurisdiction over the younger knights.

Cantaro, pl. Cantari: Unit of weight in Mediterranean region; *cantaro forfori*=ca. 92 heavy Venetian lbs., *cantaro levedi*=ca. 128 heavy Venetian lbs., and the *cantaro gervi*=ca. 200 heavy Venetian lbs.

Capitão, Capitão-mor: Captain or (higher-ranking) Captain-Major, with charge over naval and military forces in a particular locale or expedition.

Cartaz: A safe-conduct pass for navigation in the Indian Ocean issued by the Portuguese to non-Portuguese ships.

There was a fee for the pass, and those ships intercepted without one were liable to confiscation.

Cavaleiro: Knight, lower-ranking noble.

Commenda: Commandery; revenue-yielding land grant made to knights or members of the military orders in reward for their services.

Commendador: Commander in the Military Orders; knight holding revenue yielding lands or commanderies.

Commendador-mor: Chief Commander in various Military Orders charged with administering the Order's commanderies.

Cruzado, pl. Cruzados: Portuguese gold coin worth 380 *reís* down to 1499; from 1499–1517 the rate was 390 *reís*; and thereafter 400 *reís*.

Degredado: Convict who was allowed to commute his sentence with exile and service overseas in the empire.

Dom: A status title in the nobility, from the Latin *dominus*.

Estado da India: "State of India"; Portuguese settlements in Indian Ocean basin from East Africa to South China sea, eventually administered from Goa.

Fanão, pl. Fanôes: A coin at Calicut worth ca. 25 *reís* in about 1500.

Fidalgo: A high-ranking noble; literally *filho de algo*, "son of somebody," who held patents of nobility granted by the king.

Foro: Charter granting a right or privilege.

Mappilas: Muslim community on the Kerela coast of India and Calicut.

Mestre: Master; the title given to the head of the various Military Orders.

Misqâl, pl. misqâls: A gold coin worth approximately 470 *reís*.

Nau: A large, usually three-master ship, a carrack.

Padrão, pl. Padrões: Stone columns inscribed with the royal crest of Portugal, which were erected along the route of discovery along the African coast and India.

Portolani: Originally medieval pilot books containing maps with coastlines, harbors, and rivers' mouths that by the fifteenth century had evolved into practical coastal navigational charts. In English, these nautical guides were known as rutters, in Portuguese as *roteiros*.

Quintal: A unit of weight equal to 128 lbs.

Real, pl. Reís or Reais: Portuguese silver coin whose exchange rate varied from 380 (to 1499), to 390 (1499–1517) to 400 (1517–) to the *cruzado*.

Reconquista: The Reconquest of the Iberian peninsula from the Moors or Islamic rule.

Regimento: Official act or standing order.

Roteiro, pl. Roteiros: Rutters, or sailing instructions with detailed nautical information for a particular route.

Sisas do sal: Excise tax on salt.

Tença: Annual pension granted by the Crown.

Vedor da Fazenda: The Controller-general of finance. The second most powerful official in the bureaucracy of the *Estado da India* after the Viceroy.

Xerafim, pl. xerafins: Originally, a silver coin at Calicut equal to 2 *fanões* in gold or 300 *reís*; later a silver coin minted in Goa with the same value; probably from the Persian *ashrafi*.

Index